VOL. I

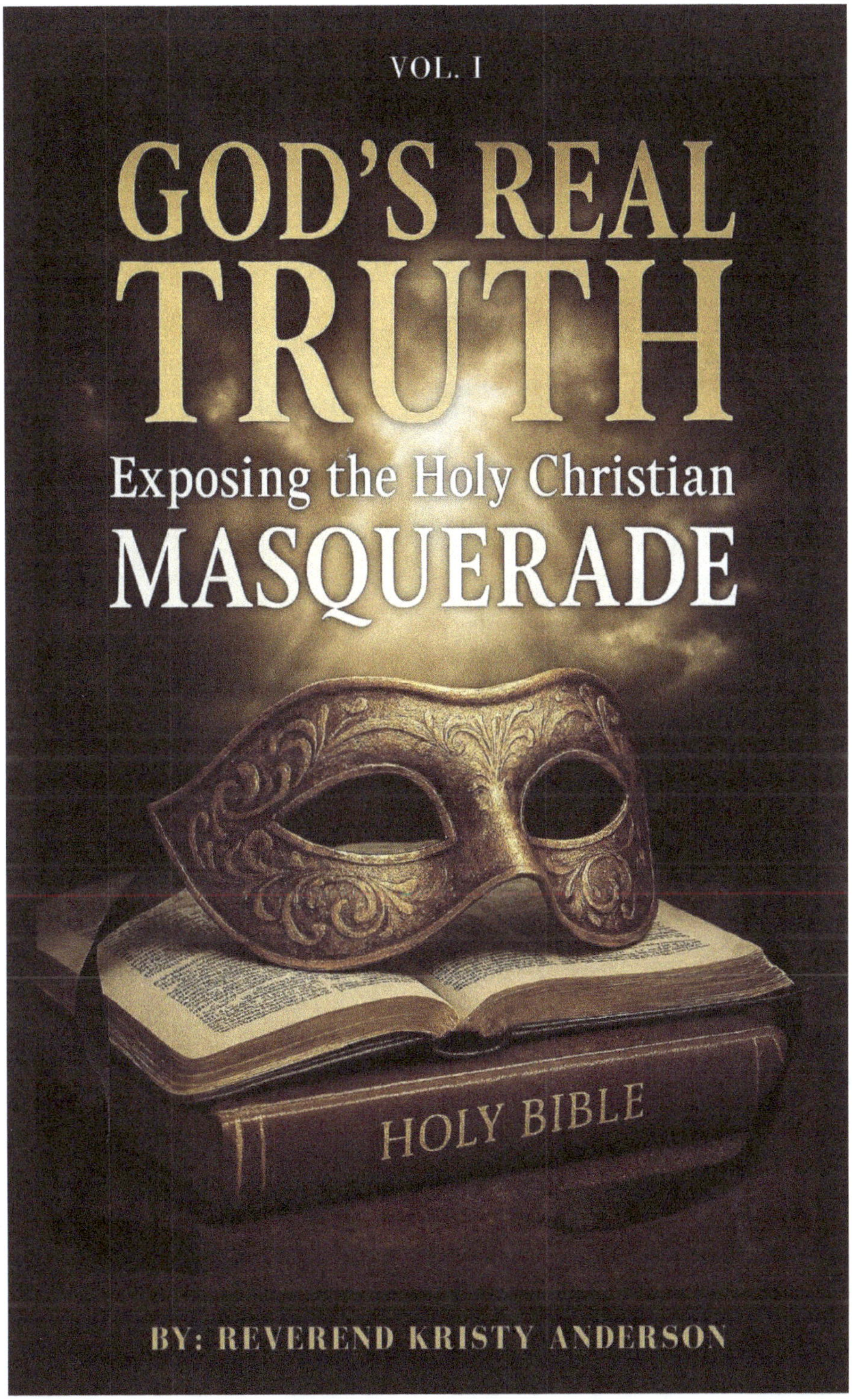

GOD'S REAL TRUTH

Exposing the Holy Christian

MASQUERADE

HOLY BIBLE

BY: REVEREND KRISTY ANDERSON

Printed in the United States of America
First Printing, 2025
ISBN 979-8-90046-740-5

I'm a preacher and author who gives her books away so I don't make much money. Thus, I have not been able to renew my website premium plan so I cannot use my regular domain at the moment. My website is still active under the following domain and you can find download links to my books on the website.

https://authorkristyanders.wixsite.com/taboo-truths

Once I am able to renew my plan my regular domain will be used again. Thus, if the link above does not work use the following link below

www.tabootruths.org

Make sure to subscribe to my website for all the lates news and blogs.

This Book is Dedicated to God, YHWH Allah,

And his Real True Chosen People

All 144,000 of the. Hold on it won't

Be much longer before pain is gone and

Peace finally comes. We will build the true

Zion very, very soon.

Contents

"When God sends to men warnings so important that they are represented as proclaimed by holy angels flying in the midst of heaven, He requires every person endowed with reasoning powers to heed the message. The fearful judgments denounced against the worship of the beast and his image, should lead all to a diligent study of the prophecies to learn what the mark of the beast is, and how they are to avoid receiving it. But the masses of the people turn away their ears from hearing the truth, and are turned unto fables."

-Ellen Gould Harmon White

Prolog

In 2018 I died in a car accident. God gave me a second chance to come back and spread his real truth to the world. Since my accident God shows and tells me things. Before my accident I was a born and raised Christian. Thus, I understand Christian beliefs and the trinity just fine. However, the things God was showing and telling me didn't match my Christian beliefs.

Since the things he was showing and telling me didn't match my Christian beliefs I began to read a lot. I was on a mission to understand the things God showed me. The only way to understand it was to read. Before I knew it I had read my bible front to back multiple times, almost every sacred text on the ancient text archive, the lost and missing books of the Bible, and very many philosophy books.

It wasn't long before I understood what God showed me but I still desired to learn more and more. Thus, I enrolled in school to study theology. In school the things I learned matched things God showed me yet some of my professors and classmates would over look these things or form explanations that would fit the Christian belief that was opposite of what we was learning and what the Bible actually stated.

I did very well in school. I was on the dean's list multiple years. My high GPA earned me a membership into Omega Nu Lambda Honors Society and a spot on the student advisory board. I also wrote for the online school News Paper. In my senior year, which is when I really started expressing my beliefs and opinion when others would look over facts, my financial aid was snatched from me.

I began to face antisemitism at school for my views from some professors and from many classmates. However, there were a few professors and classmates that loved my daringness and unique essays. The antisemitism really showed when the school began to block me for funds I was qualified for and scholarships I deserved to graduate.

They did still allow me to finish all my theology courses to run up my student account bill by giving me false hopes of receiving funds needed to graduate. These Christian universities are head of the game when it comes to the Christian religion. They have even turned theology, what should be the study of God, into the study of the Christian religion.

They may have stopped me from receiving their stupid piece of paper that they call a degree but I still have my transcript and I am a theologian, whether they want to admit it or not.

I am also an ordained reverend as well but I am not a member of any religion. I simply follow God and his truth which is what we are all supposed to do.

However, the founders and leaders of Christianity have created this huge illusion to make people think they are following God and his truth when they are truly not. That is why God has mad me write this book. To deliver his real truth to as many people as possible before disaster comes.

We are living in days that are worse than the days of Noah. People today change Gods word to fit whatever is popular in society but it just doesn't work that way and never has. Just as God reset the world in the days of Noah, he is about to do it again and only 144,000 people will be saved, they are the chosen. Do you realize how small of a number that is in a world where there is billions of Christians? That should show you all that something isn't right.

This book is the word of God that he has spoken/written through me. I am a true seeing prophet of the God of Abraham, YHWH Allah. Somethings in this book may sound a littler familiar to people who know some gnostic text. It may sound familiar to some people who know video games and mythology. There are bits and pieces of truth in the world but Christianity and Science has blinded you all from seeing it.

Though, some things in this book may seem familiar to some who know the things listed above, you will have never heard this whole complete story of God's real truth. I swear to you every bit of it is real and I have proved myself before.

The first part of this book will seem very different to Christians, if it helps read the first part as a fairy tale and when you get to the second part of this book it will all make sense to you.

I know I will probably get a lot of hate for this book but hate me all you want. All publicity is good publicity and they more you talk bad about it the more the word about it will spread. Thus, the more that will be curious and read it. If you hate this one your definitely going to hate vol ii of this book. However, I am a true reverend. I do not care to save feelings, God has sent me to attempt to help save souls.

I do not care what this world allows to be written, said, or published. I live by God's law not the worlds and no one will shut me up when God tells me to speak. I will never stop excising my right to freedom of speech and to publish nor will I ever stop standing up against what is wrong or for what is right. Mortal men have began to overstep boundaries when it comes to control especially when it comes to what you can and can not say.

I will never water down truth to make a mortal human feel better about their dirty deeds. There is a difference between judging someone and preaching what is right. These preachers today should be ashamed of themselves for doing just that because by doing so you jeopardize people's salvation.

I will not beg anyone to believe me either because it is just my job to deliver the message. You can do what you want with it. I will however, treat everyone kindly and do my best to help anyone who don't understand, understand truth better. If you have any questions after reading this book about anything, feel free to message me at tabootruths.ka@gmail.com.

The True Story of the
Bride, Creation, and Purpose of Life

Chapter 1: The Creation of Barbelo (the Mother) and the Son

1.1 God All Alone

In the boundless expanse of existence, there was only **God**—alone and bored to say the least, with no one to share His infinite love. All He wanted was someone to share his love with that would in turn love him as well. God wanted a family but not just any family. He desired a family that wasn't perfect but at the same time was perfect for him.

This would not be an easy fast process. It would take time and a lot of work and love. He didn't care though. God wanted his family and He would do what needed to be done to have a family of his own. Certain events had to unfold first; this would not be a swift process, but one that would be worth every moment.

And so, God got right to work.

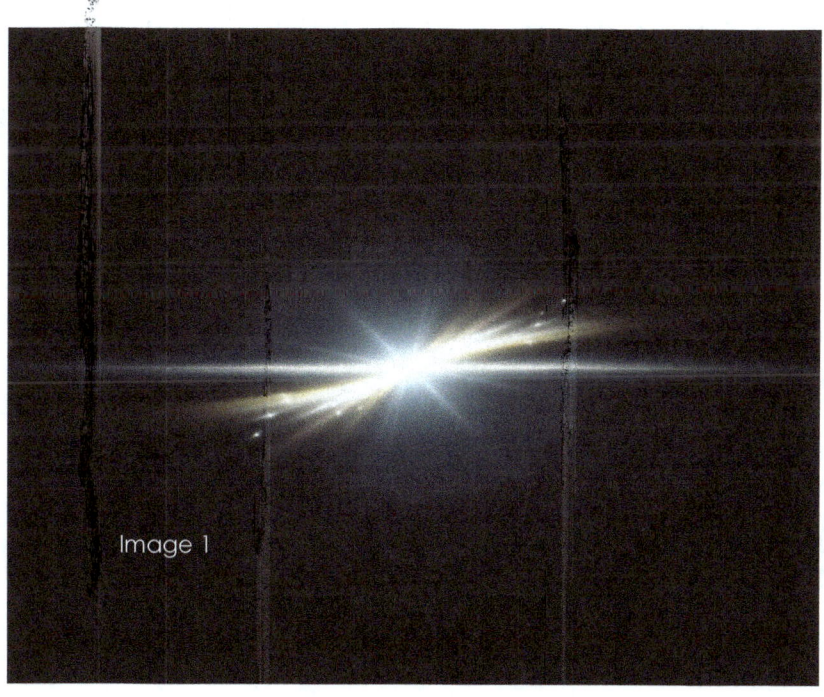

Image 1

Image one above is an AI created image of a representation of what God looks like. This is the best representation I could get because God is to glorious and beautiful to fully picture or describe.

1.2 The Creation of Barbelo

The first to emerge from His divine **imagination** was Barbelo, His female counterpart. A counterpart, much like what humans call a husband or wife, but so much more. Barbelo was the very essence of what He had dreamed—His perfect match. Though she was made in His image, no being could ever be equal to God. Only He, known now as **YHWH.** to the Hebrews and **Allah** to the Islamic community, reigns as the one true God. But **Barbelo** was everything He desired, and He loved her beyond measure.

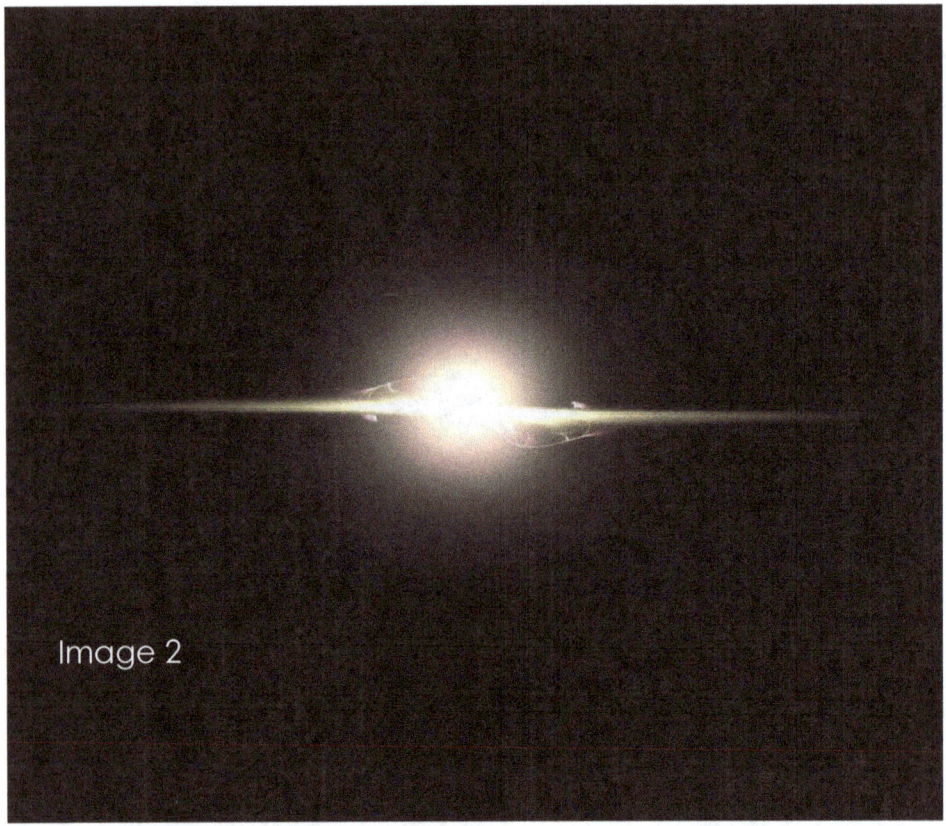

Image 2

The same goes for image 2 as image one. This is only an AI generated representation of what the Mother Barbelo looks like.

1.3 The Creation of the Son

Overwhelmed with gratitude for her own existence and the love He showed her, Barbelo yearned to create something for Him in return. She wanted to create an offspring, for God. She was so amazed that it was her that he had designed and created for himself to give his love too.

The only way that she co
uld thank him for loving her so much was to create for him an offspring made from their love.

God already knew she would desire to do this because he planned for her to do so when he created her which is why he created her. Her making him an offspring was all a part of his bigger plan to create for him and Barbelo both the perfect family.

Yet, Barbelo understood something critical: though she wished to surprise Him, she must first seek His approval. She knew that God was the ultimate authority. She knew that all things must be done according to his will instead of her own because he alone was **omniscience**, all knowing. Thus, God knows best so we must all seek his approval before making decisions.

She could still surprise him though if he promised not to look at what she was creating until it was finished. God agreed that she could go a little ways from him to create it as long as she didn't go too far from him. God also promised her he wouldn't peek until she completed his offspring.

With His blessing, Barbelo hurried away, her heart racing with anticipation. She poured herself into her creation, carefully considering each trait, each characteristic that her offspring would need. And each time she asked God to allow her to use a **characteristic** he approved her request.

Then, at last, her work was complete.

Eagerly, Barbelo returned to Him, leading God to the place where she had formed their first offspring. The moment He laid eyes upon His son; joy radiated from Him—so powerfully that a spark leapt forth and struck the child's spirit. In an instant, life surged through the son, igniting his being. Alive, just as his father and mother before him.

And his first act, in the presence of God and Barbelo, was to offer gratitude. For bringing him into existence, for loving him before he was even formed.

Chapter Two: The Son Creates Hakmah Sophia, His Bride/Counterpart

2.1 The Son Creates His Bride Hakma Wisdom Sophia

The Son was granted permission from God to create freely, shaping existence as he wished. God, knowing that Barbelo had asked for characteristics that built a loving, kind, good, and humble being allowed the Son to create as he pleased. Of course, God already knew that the Son would want to create and he would need to in order for God to finally get His most perfect family that He imagined.

The first creation of the son was **Hakmah Wisdom—Sophia**. She became his bride, his perfect **counterpart**—the **bride** of the **bridegroom**. Sophia was the most breathtaking creation across the heavens and the earth. She was also a being of extraordinary wisdom, beauty, and kindness. Yet, possessing **wisdom** does not always mean one follows it.

Watching the Son craft wonders for God, their mother, and herself, Sophia felt a longing of her own—a desire to create. Just as Barbelo had once created the Son for God, Sophia wished to bear an offspring for the Son.

However, there was one thing she wanted most of all: to surprise him with her creation. Sophia adored the tale of the creation of the Son and his brothers the **archangels**. She listened eagerly whenever Barbelo told her the story of how she and God created her bridegroom, always wanting to hear more and never wanting the story to end.

Yet, one detail was always missing—Barbelo never told Sophia that she had first sought God's permission. Barbelo left that out of the story for a good reason.

God shared everything with Barbelo, including His grand design for the perfect family He would grant her. And so, Barbelo deliberately left out the part about seeking divine counsel, knowing that, in order for God's plan to unfold, Sophia would have to act alone.

Thus, Sophia decided to create an offspring—without telling her counterpart and without his help.

Beyond the thrill of the surprise, an uncertainty nagged at her. She feared that he would not yet allow her to create an offspring due to him believing that she was not yet ready to do so. She had studied him closely. Sophia would observe how he breathed life into the heavens. She understood his process and believed that, if she followed his example, nothing could go wrong.

Chapter Three: Sophia Creates Yaldabaoth

3.1 Sophia Self Reproduces Yaldabaoth

While the son was immersed in creation, Sophia quietly slipped away. She believed she had found a place beyond his sight—a hidden space where she could bring forth an offspring of her own. What she didn't realize was that the son knew exactly what she was doing. Yet, he did nothing to stop her.

He, like his mother Barbelo, understood that this was all part of God's greater plan. God's perfect family was also his perfect family, and its existence relied on Sophia taking these actions.

Once she was believed she was beyond his watchful eye, Sophia initiated the process of self-reproduction, forging an offspring without her counterpart's consent. But the moment the creation was complete, dread gripped her heart. Something was terribly wrong.

3.2 The First Being of Matter

Unlike the radiant beings of heaven, who were adorned in the glorious light of God, this creature was monstrous—grotesque and unsettling in form. And beyond its hideous appearance, it possessed something no other heavenly being had ever held: a physical body. She had never seen anything quite like it before.

In heaven, God, Barbelo, the Son, the archangels, and Hakmah were beings of pure Godly light. If one were to reach out and touch them, there would be nothing to feel—no physical substance, only divine presence. But this offspring, the one Sophia had created, was different. If touched, it could be physically felt. It had weight, form—a stark contrast to the ethereal existence of the celestial realm.

3.3 Sophia Begins to Feel guilt and Shame

Guilt, shame, and panic surged through Sophia.

She had gone against divine order and made a creation unlike anything else. She was in great distress since she was unaware that her actions were part of God's design.

Fear clouded her judgment. Without hesitation, she seized the monstrous being, flung it deep into the depths of chaos casting it away from the heavens to the very bottom of the void that was below.

Desperate to conceal her mistake, she set the beast upon a throne and named it Yaldabaoth. Then, she encased it within a great dome or **firmament** as some call it, covering it with a thick, impenetrable fog—hoping, praying, that no one in the heavens would ever lay eyes upon what she had done.

Chapter Four: Yaldabaoth Takes Sophia's Light Leaving Her Stuck Below the Heavens

4.1 Sophia Stuck Below Her Place in the Heavens

With a weary sigh, Sophia completed her task, covering the dome in a thick fog, hoping that no one in the heavens would ever glimpse at what she has thrown down to the very bottom of chaos. Her heart heavy, she turned to ascend back to her rightful place in the high heavens. But as she began her journey upward, she noticed something was wrong.

Each attempt to rise felt like an invisible force was pulling her down. Panic crept into her chest. Struggling against the weight of her mistake, she tried again. No matter how hard she tried, she could ascend no higher.

Frantic, she drifted back and forth over the creation she had no intentions of creating. The creation would become known as Earth, the domain she had built for Yaldabaoth. And as she gazed upon him, horror washed over her.

A brilliant light shone above his head, unmistakable in its radiance. It was her light, the light of God, her power. Without enough power you cannot rise to the Heavens.

4.2 Sophia's Light Taken While Giving Birth

Only now did she understand—Yaldabaoth had taken it unknowingly at his birth. Since she had created him without her counterpart, he had absorbed more than half the light she once possessed.

When making offsprings with a counterpart each being gives the offspring some of its light. This keeps things balanced so that each being along with its offspring has enough light to go wherever they please to go in the heavens or below.

She was homesick and feared she would never be able to make it back to the heavens and even worse- never see God or her bridegroom again.

Dread consumed her.

What had she done?

How could she fix this?

Regret clawed at her soul, pressing down with an unbearable weight. She had been blinded by her desire, unaware of the consequences that would follow. Now, with only a small remnant of her light, she could no longer reach the highest heaven. She had lost her place.

Loneliness set in like a shadow.

 Sorrow quickly overtook her. She cried out in such great despair that he voice was heard in the heavens. However, God already had his eyes on her. He knew where she was and never took his eyes off her. He loved her she was his daughter.

Barbelo, wished that he could just bring her home right then but it wasn't yet time.

Chapter 5: Yaldabaoth Believes he is God and Begins to Create

5.1 Yaldabaoth Believes He is God and Begins to Create

Yaldabaoth awoke for the first time to a vast emptiness. There was no mother, no father, no other being in sight. Nothing. Alone in the void, he drew the only conclusion his mind could fathom—he must be God.

With this belief in his heart, Yaldabaoth began to create. But unlike the radiant beings of the heavens, his creations were made of matter—dense, tangible forms that lacked the divine essence of the true God. He commanded each creation to call him God, demanding their worship and unwavering devotion.

5.2 Yaldabaoth Demands His Creations to Call Him God

Meanwhile, Sophia drifted through the heavens, crying out for help, searching for any who could hear her plea. While drifting to and fro over the waters of the earth she heard the demands that Yaldabaoth was giving to the beings that he had created in such a short time.

She could not let this go on any longer. For the first time she decided that she had to make herself known to Yaldabaoth. She had no choice because he now believed he was God and she knew that no one is to be called God but God. However, she kept in mind that he knew no better at the moment. For he believed he was the only being when he woke up after being created.

5.3 Sophia Reveals Herself to Yaldabaoth

As she slowly approached him to make herself known she could still hear his voice echoing through the vast expanse, issuing his command to those he had made: to worship him as God.

Without further hesitation, she confronted him, rebuking him with firm but kind words to try and explain to him what had happened. She told him the truth. She explained to him that he was not the first to exist that in fact there were many beings that already existed in the heavens.

She then informed him that it was she who was his mother and his creator, but she, too, had a creator, one formed by the true God, YHWH Allah. She explained that the One through whom all things were made was a jealous God but loving God. No one, under any circumstances, should ever claim the title of God for themselves.

Sophia the pleaded for what she had lost, her light. She needed to return to her place in the high heavens. To do so, she needed her light back. She explained this to him and promised to see God about giving him light and letting him come to the highest heavens with the rest of the heavenly beings.

She knew God was loving and forgiving and would forgive her if she told him what she done and was truly sorry for doing so.

But did Yaldabaoth care?

Did he listen to the truth she spoke?

No. He did not.

Chapter 6: Sabaoth Rebukes His Father Yaldabaoth and Dethrones Him

6.1 Yaldabaoth's First Created Son Rebukes and Dethrones Him

Yaldabaoth erupted in fury, refusing to acknowledge the existence of another God. His rage consumed him, a storm of denial and defiance.

He would not accept that he was anything less than the supreme being. His wrath shook creation itself.

But amid his fury, his son—Sabaoth—saw something his father had failed to recognize the glory of God.

He had heard Sophia's words, her rebuke against Yaldabaoth, and though fear gripped him, something stirred within. He stepped forward, trembling yet determined to rebuke his father.

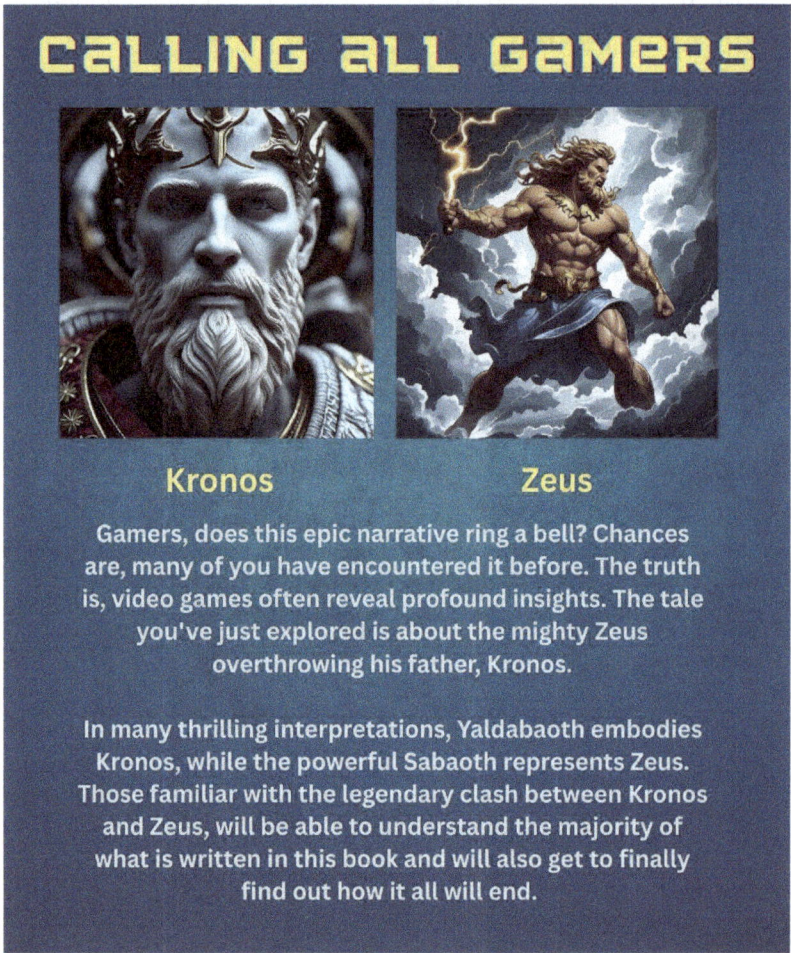

CALLING ALL GAMERS

Kronos   **Zeus**

Gamers, does this epic narrative ring a bell? Chances are, many of you have encountered it before. The truth is, video games often reveal profound insights. The tale you've just explored is about the mighty Zeus overthrowing his father, Kronos.

In many thrilling interpretations, Yaldabaoth embodies Kronos, while the powerful Sabaoth represents Zeus. Those familiar with the legendary clash between Kronos and Zeus, will be able to understand the majority of what is written in this book and will also get to finally find out how it all will end.

He had never challenged his father before, never dared to defy the being that ruled over him. But now, with the radiance of God illuminating his understanding, he could not remain silent.

Despite his terror, he rebuked his father.

Yaldabaoth did not yield easily. He fought, determined to hold his throne, to keep his false dominion intact. But he underestimated the strength of his son's conviction. The battle raged, but in the end, Yaldabaoth was overthrown.

6.2 God Rewards the Son of Yaldabaoth, Sabaoth for His Faith

God saw it all.

He saw Sabaoth's courage, his loyalty, his unwavering faith. He watched as Sabaoth stood against falsehood in defense of the truth.

And so, as a reward, God lifted Sabaoth into the heavens—not the highest heavens but to the heaven above the earth.

God allowed Sabaoth to rule over the heaven above the earth, the airs of the earth, and all things and beings that walk on the earth. He was favored by God due to Sabaoth having faith in Him though he had never even saw Him.

God also rewarded the celestial beings that assisted Sabaoth with dethroning his father. He brought them up the earth's heaven and allowed them to assist Sabaoth with his ruling. Sabaoth quickly became Gods most favorite of all the celestial beings that Yaldabaoth created.

Chapter 7: Getting Sophia's Light Back: The Purpose of Adam

7.1 The Plan to Get Sophia's Light Back

Once Sabaoth was placed in the heavens, God gave him a crucial command—he was to assist Sophia in recovering her stolen light from Yaldabaoth and ensure the plan unfolded safely.

Sophia, filled with wisdom, knew exactly what needed to be done. A human would be created, and the angels would have to deceive Yaldabaoth into transferring Sophia's light into this new being, man named Adam.

This would be done by telling Yaldabaoth to blow life into Adam's mouth. Life only comes from the light of God. Thus, once he blew into Adam's mouth the light would be transferred from Yaldabaoth to Adam.

Upon the Adam's death, Sophia's light would be released, allowing it to be collected and returned to her. Once restored, her spirit could inhabit flesh, die, and ascend once more to the highest heavens—her rightful place.

7.2 The Creation of Adam

The deception was simple.

The angels imagined how they wanted to shape Adam. Thus, they shaped man in their own imagination (Image). They crafted Adam from red clay. They named him Adam which meant red due to the color of his skin being the same as red clay.

 Once they completed the molding of Adam into a man they presented him before Yaldabaoth. They told Yaldabaoth they had made a being powerful enough to dethrone YHWH and his son Sabaoth who God placed over the heavens of Earth and all things on earth, so that Yaldabaoth may become God.

Of course, this was just a made-up story to trick Yaldabaoth because they knew that was what Yaldabaoth wanted most.

The angels told Yaldabaoth that the only thing required to bring Adam to life was Yaldabaoth's breath. If he blew into Adam's mouth, they promised, the new creation would rise and overthrow YHWH.

However, they knew that when Yaldabaoth blew his breath into Adam the light of God, YHWH Allah, that Sophia once possessed would then be transferred to Adam

7.3 Yaldabaoth Blows the Light/Life of God into Adam

Blinded by ambition, Yaldabaoth wasted no time. He examined the new creature that the angels he created had made. Yaldabaoth gave them his approval. He was desperate to become greater than YHWH. Thus, he believed the lie that was told to him.

Leaning down he put his mouth to Adam's and he exhaled Sophia's light straight into Adam, and in that moment, Adam awoke. Yaldabaoth was amazed when he realized that Adam was now a living, breathing being.

Now, all that was required was time. Adam had to live and eventually die of old age to return Sophia's light to the heavens. It was a flawless plan—until Yaldabaoth discovered the truth.

7.4 Yaldabaoth Discovers He Has Been Tricked

Realizing he had been deceived, he devised a wicked countermeasure. First, he placed a spell upon Adam. The spell he placed on Adam put him in a trance like state so that Adam only knew Yaldabaoth. He was not conscious to anything outside the garden.

Yaldabaoth put this spell on him because if he only knew Yaldabaoth then the light of Sophia that came from God would return to Yaldabaoth upon the death of Adam. The angels saw that Yaldabaoth put this spell on Adam so they come up with another plan.

They decided to mold a woman from clay and the rib of Adam since it contained the light of the bride which would be needed to bring the women, Eve, to life. Once she was a living being she could then teach Adam who God was since she was not under Yaldabaoth's spell.

When Yaldabaoth realized they had created Eve he felt his control slipping. He was filled with rage and thought of another plan—a darker, more insidious trick.

He decided he would create children with Eve. If she bore his offspring, the bright light within her would be tainted with evil—diluted by his own dimmed essence.

7.5 Eve Gives Birth to Cain and Able

Sure, enough Eve birthed two sons, Cain and Abel, the human children of Yaldabaoth. Though, many believed they belonged to Adam, Adam did not produce a child in his own likeness until Seth was born.

From the beginning, Cain harbored a shadow in his heart—for he was born of darkness. The evil and Jealousy in Yaldabaoth was also in Cain. Able on the other hand had more of Sophia's light that come from God in Him.

Eventually the evil in Cain over took him and he killed his brother Able.

Able's blood sank deep into the earth creating a pact with death through the sin of murder. This pact with death would require every spirit and soul/light in a person's flesh to go down to Sheol at death instead of returning to God.

God would now have to create his own people to get the Bride's light back so she may return home. So, God allowed Adam to father a son named Seth in the likeliness of Adam.

As Genesis 5:3 states,

"And Adam lived one hundred and thirty years, and begat a son in his own likeness, after his image, and named him Seth."

The descendants of Seth were meant to remain pure, carrying forth the Bride's radiant light. Yet, over time, even they would fall under the influence of Cain's bloodline.

Chapter 8: The Fall of the Watchers

8.1 The Daughters of Man Become Beautiful

After Cain's transgression against Abel and before Seth's arrival, Cain took his sister as his wife. Together, they abandoned Adam and Eve, settling in the land of Nod—a place of exile and wandering. Their offspring, born of incest, were deemed **unnatural**, a consequence still observed in individuals from such unions today.

Time passed, and Adam fathered Seth. Eventually, the descendants of Cain and Seth encountered one another. Over **generations**, their **bloodlines** began to intermingle, slowly diminishing the effects of incest. And as those incest traits faded from the blood of man, the daughters of men became beautiful.

8.2 The Son's of God aka The Watchers

As humanity multiplied, God appointed certain of His sons to serve as **Watchers**—known as the **Sons of God**, or simply, **the Watchers**. Their divine duty was to observe mankind, ensuring that events unfolded as intended so that Sophia's light could one day be reclaimed and she could return to her rightful place in the heavens with her bridegroom.

This was all part of God's grand design. He knew Sophia's restoration would take time—thousands upon thousands of human years. The Watchers would safeguard the process, maintaining order. At first, their mission was easy to say the least, for the daughters of men had not yet become so beautiful. But when their beauty emerged, **temptation** crept into the hearts of the Watchers, complicating their purpose.

8.3 The Lust of Semeyjaza

Among them, Semeyjaza was appointed as their leader. After seeing the daughters of man become so pleasing to his eyes, he couldn't control his **lust**. His desire for the daughters of men burned hotter than any of the Watchers. He yearned for a human woman, longing to take one as his bride and even worse bear children with her, despite knowing such an act would be a betrayal of God.

God had warned them of this very temptation when He entrusted them with their task. He pleaded with them not to take on such a task making sure they knew what would be come of it. Still, Semeyjaza begged him to let him do the task at hand assuring God that he would stay loyal to him.

One day Semeyjaza decided he couldn't take the lust any longer. He had to act on this feeling of lust that consumed him. Finally, he decided he couldn't t take it any longer and devised a plan to get some of the other watchers to commit this sinful act with him.

8.4 Semeyjaza's Plan to Descend to Earth and Marry a Daughter of Man to Produce Offspring

He decided he and his fellow watchers would descend to Earth, each Watcher that come down to the earth would claim a daughter of man as his wife, and father children with her. There was no way the other watchers wouldn't agree to do this with him. Semeyjaza knew that they lusted after the daughters of man too.

The images above show the actual real mount Hermon and where it is located on the map.

Semeyjaza gathered the Watchers who harbored the same forbidden desire. He presented his plan to the Watchers, and they listened excitedly.

Enthusiasm grew among them, and one by one, they pledged to carry it out together. To ensure loyalty, Semeyjaza bound them with an oath—a pact that none could break.

8.5 The Fall of the Watchers

And so, the Watchers fell.

Semeyjaza, his second-in-command Azazel, and the others descended to Earth, landing upon Mount Hermon. Two hundred Watchers came down, abandoning their duty. Semeyjaza and Azazel divided them into ten groups, each consisting of twenty, appointing a leader to oversee them.

Each of the Watchers took a daughter of man as a bride. But their union was far from ordinary—these fallen angels did not simply take wives; they revealed to them the secrets of heaven.

They taught them the mysteries that men had long sought—how to cast spells, divine the unseen, master alchemy. They showed them how to forge weapons, adorn their faces with makeup, pierce their flesh, craft jewelry, and much more.

Every hidden truth, every celestial mystery forbidden to mankind, was laid bare before the daughters of men.

Many people today are scared of dying and I believe it is because they think heaven will be boring. However, heaven will be far from boring. I know because I have saw just a glimpse of it with my own two eyes. We also know it isn't boring because it was the secrets of heaven that were taught to man by the Sons of God.

What that means is many of the things we know and do today are secrets of heaven. It was bad for the Sons of God to teach us these things because when used wrongly by bad people these things of heaven can cause chaos. You can look at the world today and see proof of that with your own two eyes.

8.6 The Giant Offspring of the Watchers and Daughters of Man

Not only did the Watchers reveal the secrets of heaven to man but they also did the unimaginable and bore offspring as the originally planned, with the daughters of man. The consequence of having children with the daughters on man was dire. Just as Wisdom Sophia's creation had been unnatural, so too were the children born from the Watchers and mortal women.

The daughters of men birthed monstrous beings—giants, grotesque and terrible. Known as the Nephilim, these creatures were not merely large; they were filled with wickedness. They ravaged the earth, sinned against both man and beast, consuming all the earth's resources that were essential for survival.

Their corruption spread. The giants not only sinned against man but also against beast, twisting the creatures of the land into enormous, fearsome beasts—what would later be known as dinosaurs.

Blood soaked the earth.

Man fell, beasts perished, and the cries of the devoured rose from Sheol below. Their suffering echoed through the heavens, reaching the ears of the angels. Through sin man had now made a deal with death and Sheol received every soul once their life on earth was completed, even the souls of the Saint.

This meant that none of Sophia's light could be collected until the souls were freed from Sheol which would require a man to defeat death by not sinning.

And the angels, hearing their desperate pleas, turned to God—for justice, for mercy, for the souls lost to the horrors unleashed upon the world.

Chapter 9: Enoch, The Son of Man and God

9.1 Enoch the Son of Man

During the era when fallen angels and giants roamed the Earth, one man stood apart—a righteous and sinless soul untouched by corruption. His name was **Enoch**, the seventh from Adam and the great-great-grandfather of **Noah**. He despised the wickedness that spread like poison, the sin that tainted mankind, the destruction wrought by the Watchers and the Giants upon humanity, animals, the earth, and even each other.

Unable to bear the weight of such overwhelming depravity, Enoch withdrew from the world. He hid himself away on a remote mountain known only to the fallen angels, seeking solitude, seeking God the forgiveness of God.

You see Enoch was a special man that was granted an extraordinary **spiritual gift**—the ability to receive divine visions and commune directly with the Almighty. He was a mediator between God and the Watchers.

The Watchers knew of Enoch's connection to God. They knew that he was the man to get their messages to God. They also knew that they were in very much trouble after seeing all the evil and destruction their sons, the Giants, had done to the earth and man.

In their desperation, they pleaded with him, hoping he could **intercede** on their behalf. When they learned of God's fury—His wrath over their corruption, over the monstrous giants they had created—they grasped at the last shred of hope. They wrote a letter to YHWH Allah, in hopes that Enoch would deliver it to him.

They feared their punishment was near. Their actions had disrupted the divine plan, delaying the bride's return to her rightful place in the heavens. If Enoch could appeal to God, persuade Him to forgive them and their offspring, perhaps their fate would change. So, Enoch went to God on behalf of the Sons of God.

9.2 YHWH Allah's Reply to the Sons of God

But when God answered, His decree was absolute.

There would be no forgiveness.

Through Enoch, God declared that the Watchers would bear witness to the downfall of their own sons. The **Nephilim**—those mighty yet grotesque creations—would turn upon each other, destroying themselves in bloodshed until each and every one of them were dead.

9.3 God Answers the Cries of the Human Souls that the Giants Devoured

The angels also carried the cries of all the souls of men up to God in the heavens around the same time that Enoch delivered the letter of the Sons of God to God. God was enraged at all the evil that has been taken place. Yes, it was all his plan but he did not plan for the angels to be unloyal to him and create the Nephilim. Thus, God had no other choice there had to be a master reset.

At once God gave commands to the loyal angels, his archangels, to deal with the problem at hand.

Gabriel was commanded to execute justice upon the *"bastards, the outcast, and the children of fornication,"* as recorded in the Book of Enoch.

Raphael was instructed to bind Azazel within a jagged, dark canyon and to cover him with rocks so that he may not see the light of day until God was ready to issue him judgement.

Michael was charged with imprisoning Semeyjaza and the rest of the Watchers, sealing them within the second heaven.

The punishments were to be carried out only after the Watchers watched their children slaughter one another. When the Giants finally kill one another, their spirits would not ascend, nor would they find rest. They would linger, doomed to wander the earth in limbo until the Day of Judgment—forever known as *"evil spirits, and evil spirits they shall be."*

Enoch delivered this grim message, and the Watchers were filled with despair.

But God was not finished.

9.4 God Tells Enoch of Noah, His Descendant to Come

His angels revealed to Enoch the sacred secrets of the heavens. YHWH Allah, commanded him to record these divine revelations on a scroll, preserving them alongside a prophecy—a warning of the great flood that would come, a cataclysm that would cleanse the earth. But there was hope.

God knew that a descendant of Enoch would be born and that he would fear God and do as God commands. This man's name would be Noah and God would save Noah so that the Bride would be able to one day return home.

9.5 Enoch Taken by God to Walk with God, The First to Never Taste Death

Once his sacred task was complete, Enoch bid farewell to his kin.

And then, God took him.

At the age of 365 walked with God. Enoch did not taste death—he was spared from the sin-infested world, taken directly into the presence of the Almighty. He walked with God. And then, in a moment, he was no more.

He was the first to vanish from the earth, never knowing death—for God had taken him. God saved Enoch from death for a very important reason that we will discuss soon.

Chapter 10: Metatron, The Son and Image of God

10.1 Enoch the Son of God, Metatron

Upon being taken up into heaven, Enoch was given a new name— Metatron. Known by some as the Lesser YHWH, he was transformed by God into His son and divine image.

No longer merely a man, Metatron became a celestial being of immense power, towering above all others.

God adorned him with 36 pairs of wings, each spreading in majesty, and countless eyes covering his body. These eyes served a sacred purpose—they allowed him to see all things, to witness every action, every deed of mankind.

For Metatron had been appointed to the holiest of all beings created by YHWH Allah. He became the **Holy Scribe of God**, entrusted with recording all the deeds of men.

Elevated to back to his divine status, Metatron was seated on a throne at the right side of God Himself. He was not just transformed—he was revealed as **the Son of God**, a being of pure radiance and authority.

Nobody really knows what metatron truly looks like. However, the book of Enoch gives us a good description of how he looks. Thus, with the help of the book of Enoch and AI I was able to come up with the image above that is similar to how Metatron looks.

10. 2 Metatron the Son Created by Barbelo and God Together

But Metatron's story did not begin in that moment. He was the first to be created by Barbelo and God. He was the first Son. From his own will, Metatron formed **Hakmah Sophia**, his Bride.

He had walked the Earth first as Enoch, fulfilling his mortal purpose until God took him back into the heavens, ensuring that His son would not be lost to the corruption of mankind.

Chapter 11: Sabaoth Refuses to Bow Down to Metatron

11. 1 Sabaoth's Jealousy

Upon his transformation, God commanded all celestial beings to bow before Metatron, appointing him as ruler over all created and born beings. The heavens trembled in reverence—but not all obeyed.

One being, outraged by the decree, refused to bow. That being was Sabaoth.

Sabaoth could not bear the thought of lowering himself before what he perceived to be nothing more than a mortal man. He did not realize that Metatron had existed long before him—before every being save for God and Barbelo.

When God transformed Enoch into His image and son, He was not creating something new but restoring Metatron to the divine being he had always been.

11.2 The Fall of Satan (Sabaoth)

Sabaoth's defiance sent shockwaves through the heavens. An uproar ensued.

He challenged God, arguing just as his father, Yaldabaoth, had once argued with his own creator—the Bride, Hakmah Sophia. But as it had ended poorly for Yaldabaoth, so too would it end for Sabaoth.

In an act of rebellion, Sabaoth attempted to rise against God, as if he stood a chance of victory. But God flicked him down from the heavens with effortless force, casting him and his rebellious angels back to the earth from which they had come. They fell like meteors, like burning stars streaking through the sky.

Yehoshua states in **Luke 10:18**

"I saw Satan fall like lightning from heaven."

And then, Metatron took his place.

Seated beside God, he began to write.

Metatron, now and forever, records every deed and action of man in the divine Holy Book. And on the Day of Judgment, it is this very book that will be opened. Every soul will be judged according to its pages. It will decide who enters the Kingdom of God and who does not.

Now is the moment that I will reveal what many have misunderstood. And we will explore this in greater depth soon but for now I'll reveal it yet it will be explained in very great detail in Part two of this book.

Metatron's spirit was incarnated into the flesh of Yehoshua. There is proof of thin in the verse above, Luke 10:18.

To the Christian community, I must say this clearly—Yehoshua, whom you call Jesus, is not God and Yehoshua's name is Yehoshua not Jesus Christ.

The Christian Bible itself proclaims that Yehoshua is the incarnation of the Son of God—not God Himself. Nowhere in scripture does it declare God to be three. God is one. Although many preachers today will pick and pull verses and use them out of context to try and prove that God is three, that is just a lie.

Yet, many have come to believe in the Trinity, a doctrine shaped largely by Paul.

And this brings us to another truth.

Paul is not a true apostle.

In fact, he is the very false apostle whom the disciples warned against in their letters.

We will uncover more soon—but for now, let us return to the true story.

Chapter 12: Sabaoth Reunites with Yaldabaoth

12.1 Sabaoth (Satan) Finds His Father Yaldabaoth (the Devil)

Once cast down to Earth, Sabaoth sought out his father, Yaldabaoth. His heart burned with jealousy, his mind consumed by thoughts of vengeance—not only against God but against Metatron most of all. He believed he should have been the one transformed, the one given divine authority. What he failed to realize was that Metatron was not merely a mortal man blessed with power. He was Enoch but was now changed back to his original form, Metatron.

When Yaldabaoth beheld Sabaoth beneath the heavens, his disbelief quickly turned to dark satisfaction. Sabaoth had come to him for a reason. Sabaoth knew his father harbored a deep hatred for God, an animosity as fierce as his own—perhaps even greater. When Sabaoth revealed what had been done to him, Yaldabaoth's fury ignited. *How dare they treat his first born son the way they did-expelling him from the heavens,* Yaldabaoth thought to himself.

In his rage, Yaldabaoth seized upon a single, twisted desire—to ensure that Hakmah Sophia would never return home. He knew that making sure that Sophia never made it back to the highest heavens with her Bridegroom would be the ultimate revenge on God and Metatron.

12.2 No Worries its all Part of God's Plan and God Will Win

He thought he was clever. He was forgetting that it was God who orchestrated all things. No scheme of his could ever truly triumph against God or Metatron. But just as bakers follow recipes and chemists adhere to formulas, God, too, follows steps and procedures to create exactly what He desires.

A baker who seeks to bake and enjoy a carrot cake cannot use chocolate batter. If the ingredients are wrong, the final creation will not align with the intended design. And so it was with Sophia's return to the heavens above. God could have simply restored her light or wiped creation clean. But doing so would ruin His plan and creation of the perfect family.

His family was still being formed—some had yet to be born in the flesh, others needed refinement, having fallen victim to human sin. The world had to continue until His family was complete. Only then could Sophia's light be fully restored—only then would there be enough to return her home.

Of course, God felt awful that Sophia was sad and lonely. However, he also knew that in the end she would feel that it was all worth it. When all is revealed to Sophia in the end, God knew that she would be pleased with his actions. She would even do it all over again after seeing the grand things God was creating for Sophia, Metatron, and the rest of those in the heavens that he held so near to his very source of being.

No matter how hard Yaldabaoth and Sabaoth tried they could never defeat God. The two would never be able to ruin God's creation. They were nothing but mere puppets that were needed for creation to unfold. He gave them a fair chance and they still did not want receive his many blessings and love due to the pridefulness that drowned their very hearts and judgement.

12.3 The Two Evil Ones Plans to Corrupt and Manipulate Mankind

The two evil beings knew that they couldn't beat God himself but believed they were clever enough to still trap Sophia down below the heavens. They figured they would accomplish this by corrupting humans more than they have already been corrupted.

Yaldabaoth and Sabaoth both knew that humans could be manipulated and deceived.

And so, the two most wicked beings ever created devised a scheme. A sinister plan they did come up with. They decided to darken the light of Sophia that humans house in their flesh. Since the light is our souls, darkening the light of our soul means to turn a good soul evil.

There was also another tactic they planned to use as soon as the time was right, when the perfect human for the job would be born. Many people believe that Judas, the disciple of Yehoshua, is the darkest soul that ever walked the earth but there was a soul even darker, the false apostle. The two decided they would use the false apostle to make humans forget and worship and God other than YHWH Allah.

If people worship another God, abandoning YHWH then eventually people would forget YHWH. If people forget YHWH, then the light would still be trapped in them since no one who don't know YHWH will make it in the Kingdom. If God was forgotten completely then the Bride would never make it home and Judgement would never come.

Chapter 13: Evil Beings Desire Flesh

13.1 The Desire of Evil Spirits

From the shadowed corners of existence, evil beings linger—waiting, whispering, writhing. Yaldabaoth and Sabaoth's wicked legions claw at the veil between their world and ours, their foul hunger fixed upon human flesh. They are patient, insidious, their motives splintered into madness.

Some seek possession with purpose. They believe that by slithering into flesh, they can dim the Bride's light—dimming its glow, suffocating its radiance—so the Bride remains imprisoned, never to ascend. To them, this deception is survival and allows them to escape judgment that will result in them burning and freezing in the icy, hot, boiling lakes of fire that God has created just for them and all humans who are like these evil beings.

Others, trembling in regret, seek refuge in a lie. They believe that if they can burrow deep within the living, they can trick God Himself by masking their blackened essence with the stolen flesh of their host. But God cannot be deceived. Flesh rots, but the soul remains unmistakable. Only the soul and spirit escape this evil, material world. Thus, flesh, whether their own or stolen, will do them no good on the day of Judgment.

And then, there are the worst of them.

The most twisted, the most delighted in cruelty—the spirits that do not fear judgment, do not seek salvation. No, they seek only chaos. These spirits are sinister and manipulative. They drip with amusement, laughing from the void, delighting in their perversions, twisting minds, filling mouths with unnatural words, bending bones to their will. They do not care what awaits them beyond the abyss—not yet, anyways.

Together, they wage unholy war not only against God, but also against man— for if they sink their sharp claws into enough souls, if they drown enough divine light, then Sophia may never rise, never escape this prison of flesh and dust.

And if Sophia remains bound, the reckoning cannot come.

Judgment will stall.

And so, they persist, creeping ever closer, waiting for their chance to slip inside the flesh of those who love God the most.

Notes Page

Chapter 14: The Bride in the Flesh

14.1 The Christian Church is Not the Bride

Contrary to what many Christians believe, the church is not the Bride of Yehoshua. That title belongs only to Hakma Sophia. Just as Yehoshua once walked the earth in flesh, so will the beautiful daughter and Bride, Sophia. When she has regained most of her light, she will be incarnated into the body of a woman.

At first, the woman will not know who she is. She will be birthed into the world unaware of who she will soon become. The angels will watch over her as a child and she will be mature at a very young age. Though she will be kind and sweet she will feel she don't fit in among others.

An event will occur that will put her in a deep sleep and she will be changed when she wakes again. At first she will not notice a difference in herself but will slowly realize that she has changed in some type of way that she can't put her finger on.

She will spend the majority of her time from then on searching for answers and questioning herself. She will be a woman who has a hard time believing in herself because no human has ever believed in her. That is when God will step in and the spirits of her ancestors who await her in paradise.

14.2 The Bride Assisted on Earth by Her Bridegroom, Angelic Brothers and Sisters, and by Her Father God and Mother Barbelo

God and the spirits of her ancestors and those who are closest to her will love and support her more than any other human could. God himself and His angels will guide her, revealing her truth little by little, and teach her the things that she doesn't yet understand. Still though, she will struggle to believe in herself.

She will be taught by God and form a very close relationship with him. She will be a wise woman but also a stubborn one. She will find it very hard to believe that God chose her out of all those who are in the world. Because of this she continuously seeks validation of who she is just as Yehoshua did. Yehoshua often asked his disciples, who do you say that I am?

And just as Yehoshua was rejected in his own homeland, Sophia will not be welcomed by many in hers. She will be met with opposition, scorn, and disbelief. She will be disliked by many for no reason at all. Men and women won't care for her much because they will sense the truth and law in her and feel threatened by her because of it.

There will be some who love her unconditionally and see something special in her. Some of them will call her the woman of truth, law, and unshakable integrity. They will see her as a daring woman who has the courage to make the world remember God when no one else would.

As a spirit, she wandered, lost. As flesh, she will wrestle with existence, unable to find her place among men. No matter where she stands, she will feel like an outsider—never truly belonging, never truly fitting in. For she is not of this world—she has never walked the earth before.

Knowing this, God will send His angels to aid her, guiding her along her way, ensuring that her journey unfolds as it must. She will pass no judgment although she will tell the truth about things and people. Her nature is not one of condemnation, but of restoration. She will seek to restore the world back to the ways of God and she will see the light that is left in people whom others have cast away.

14.3 The Bride Drawn to Troubled People

The Bride will fear no man, animal or being. Though, she may get scared at times she will fear no one but her maker. This will worry those who love her. They will be scared the company she keeps will get her hurt or in trouble. Her loved ones on earth will be unable to see the care she has for those who hurt inside. They won't be able to understand that she can feel the emotional pain of others.

She will be drawn—instinctively—to the broken, the troubled, the lost. She will understand those who no one tries to understand. A listening ear she will give to those who need to vent and she will never tell their secrets. She will encourage those who try so hard to discourage her.

People close to her will worry because of the company she is known for keeping. They will not understand how she can even stand to be around certain people, those who many call black sheep. Sometimes she will wonder the same herself after so many do her so wrong. But deep within her, the answer will stir.

She will know that we can't let others affect the way we help and care for others.

She will know that their light is dimmed.

Deep in her she will feel the urge to brighten their dimmed light.

For every lost soul restored is a step closer she is to returning to her own return home.

And so, she will reach for those forgotten, for those cast aside. She will mend hearts shattered by cruel childhoods, seek out those labeled as trouble. Not to change them—but to find and brighten the light within them.

Chapter 15: The Beginning of the End

15.1 When Hakma Sophia Walks the Earth in the Flesh

When Sophia finally walks this earth in some woman's flesh the beginning of the end will begin. The people in the world will be worse than they were in the days of Noah. They will commit the most unthinkable crimes and get away with it.

Almost every ruler on this earth will be corrupt. People, mainly scientists, will try to play God and try to create beings that are different from them. The world will be full of people who think they know God but only 144,000 will truly know him and it is them who are the chosen.

There will be many bad events that happen that take out countless numbers of people. These events will range from sicknesses, wars, natural disasters, and mass murders. Those who are not chosen will destroy one another just as the giants fought each other to the death. Those who are not chosen are no different than the giants. They have also devoured each other and earth's resources.

Over a short number of years, the population will drastically decrease. While all this is going on the chosen will begin to remember who they are. No, it is not the "woke" community that I am calling the chosen so don't think that for a minute. The woke community creates illusions in their heads to fit their own beliefs.

Those who say that they were the original Ingenious of America but are not Mexican or Native American or examples of the "woke" community. They are not "woke" they are asleep trying to play out their dreams. The "woke" community does nothing but try to steal the heritage of every group of people on this earth.

I am speaking of the real chosen. The chosen are those who belong to God or have seen the light and asked to be saved by good and believe what those who were sent by YHWH himself have taught or preached. They are the ones who can get past the theories of religious leaders, theologians, philosophers, and governments. They have their own minds and think for themselves.

It is them that will not be destroyed in the events that are to come. If a tornado hits their town, it will not touch their house. If bombs are dropped, they will not hit their homes or them. They will leave through the sickness and all other trials that will begin.

The events that will take away all the evil and those who don't know God have already begun. Examples of these events are Co-Vid, LA wildfires, hurricanes, the war in Ukraine, the war on Gaza, and mass killings. Events like these will continue to take place and get worse and worse with more and more lives lost each time. Eventually only the chosen who are angels in the flesh will be left on this earth.

Those who have been taken will be refined in the lakes of fire by God. God will take them up, ring out their sins, and refine them in the lakes of fire until they have been made clean. This will not be fun for those who are taken that do not know God or who are evil.

Chapter 16: The Rebuilding of Zion

16.1 The Zionist Today are Fakes

The movement of those who survived the holocaust to the land now known as Israel is the Zion movement because the countries who decided to move them there called it the Zion movement. However, no man on this earth has the right to declare any land or movement of people Zion. The only being that has that authority is God and he damn sure wouldn't push his people, the Gazans off their land to give it to others.

Those in Israel today, although some may have some blood of Hebrews in them, are mostly not the descendants of Jacob who is God's chosen people. The descendants of Israel were scattered. They were not all nicely placed in Germany as many may believe. By the time the holocaust took place there were many people who were not Hebrew that took on the Jewish religion.

It is of the upmost importance to know that Israel did not become a country until after WWII. When Israel is mentioned in the Bible it is not referring to any land. The mention of Israel in the Bible refers to Jacob who was renamed Israel after being killed by the angel of God and returning from death after seeing God face to face.

"And God said to him, 'Your name is Jacob; no longer shall your name be called Jacob, but Israel shall be your name.' So he called his name Israel." (Genesis 35:10)

So, you see that we should not always take the side of the country Israel just because it is named Israel because man named the land Israel not God and God does not speak of a country when he says Israel. He speaks of a certain family line of people who were scattered all over the world and will be brought back together to a land of God's choosing and they will rebuild that land, not steal it, and it will then be called Zion. Zion will be in a whole different location than Israel and Palestine altogether.

16.2 The Stationing of True Prophets and the Chosen Around the World

God has stationed his true prophets as well as other chosen people of his around the world. There are very few true prophets left and very few who are chosen. Thus, not all who claim to be a prophet will be true and not all who say they are chosen are chosen.

The son of God has warned us of false prophets and teachers who come in his name his self. We must not forget that and must not believe everyone who claims to be a prophet, preacher, or teacher of God.

God will lead his prophets to chosen people around the world in some type of way shape or fashion that only he knows in order to instruct them on his truth and what to do when it is time to take action.

The chosen will believe the prophets because what they say makes sense and goes along with the prophets of the Old Testament and with the teachings of God.

A true prophet will never contradict God and their prophecies will go along with the ancient prophet's prophecies.

Those who are left will eventually contact those who are in charge that will live in the true Zion, for instruction. Instruction and truth go forth from Zion and it will come from the mouth of a woman.

It will be a woman who has kept God's law and who has stood up for God that God will appoint to be in charge until her son comes of age. When her son comes of age he will rule over Zion. There will be nothing but peace in Zion for some years.

Slowly those who were taken from the earth and refined will be born back out through those who are left on earth, the Chosen. They will be given one last chance to know God. However, they will return to their sinful ways over time. Once the chosen that were left on earth to rebuild Zion have died there will only be one left.

The woman who ruled until her son became ruler will be the last person left. She is the bride of the bridegroom. She is Hakmah Sophia. When the last good person dies she will have only a few days left on the earth until God calls her up. She will then take her rightful place in the heavens where she belongs.

Once she is safe in the heavens God's four sons will come down from the heavens and wreak havoc on those who still remain on the earth. After all have tasted death the day we all have been waiting for will finally come. The Holy book will be opened and each person's deeds will be read out to God and each being human, evil spirits, and all angles will then be judged by their works that Metatron whose spirit was incarnated in the flesh of Enoch and Yehoshua, recorded in the Holy Book of Human Works.

notes

notes

Stopping Satan's Kingdom on Earth

Phase One

Unmasking the False Apostle Paul

Introduction

Part two of this book will focus on how Yaldabaoth and Sabaoth used Paul as their first person of the New Testament time period to begin their Greate Masquerade plan in order to stir people away from God to dim their lights. If their lights are dimmed the bride will remain stuck on earth.

 God will not completely destroy the world until his daughter is home with her bridegroom. Thus, dimming the light in us would prolong their punishment and it would also aid in bringing Satan's kingdom to earth where the devil and his son could finally rule.

You will see the truth behind the books of the New Testament as well. Paul's letters were actually the first to be written of the New Testament. The letters that were written under the true apostle's names as well as the gospels were written in response to Paul's letters. More information on this will also be given in the following pages.

What I really hope you all see in this section is the difference between the teachings of Paul and God, Yehoshua, the Prophets, and the disciples. I really wanted to spend more time on this section because there are so many things I wanted to include but God is rushing me to get this out.

When a prophet doesn't do as God says he will remove their distractions one by one. Believe me I know personally. So, this is just the very quick basics but is enough for you to realize what is really going on in the Christian religion that they don't want to share with the Christian community.

 I do understand that realizing these things are hard because when I realized these things I had no one in my corner and everyone was against me except God. Thus, feel free to email me at the email I provided at the beginning of this book if you have any questions. No question is stupid, too big, or dumb. Questions is how you get to know and build a relationship with YHWH Allah.

Chapter One: Saul

1.1   Saul's Background

The individual commonly known as Paul was initially named Saul at birth. This section will refer to him as Saul. Scholarly understanding of Saul's early childhood is limited, primarily relying on New Testament texts and other ancient writings from the period. Even the circumstances surrounding his death remain uncertain, lacking definitive historical documentation regarding the time, place, and manner of his demise *(Soards, 7)*.

However, there are some facts derived from the New Testament and ancient historical texts, that provide insights into his background. Let's examine what we do know about Saul's background.

- Saul was born into a Jewish family, reportedly from the tribe of Benjamin according to his own claims in Philippians 3:5.
- At birth, he was given the Hebrew name Saul.
- He later adopted the Roman name Paul following his alleged encounter and conversion on the road to Damascus which will be discussed in detail in a moment.

1.2   A Roman Citizen

Although Saul identified as Jewish, he and his family were Roman citizens, born in the city of Tarsus in Cilicia around the year 5 AD.

Roman citizenship was a privileged status that Paul frequently utilized to his advantage during legal disputes *(Acts 22:28)*. Being a Roman citizen had many more advantages than not. Saul went to better school than Jewish people who were not Roman citizens which gave him a better education as a child.

He lived among and mingled with Romans everyday as a child. The frequent interaction with the Romans made him more comfortable with the Romans and in turn they saw him as "part of the family" or a friend.

His frequent interactions with Romans growing up and his upbringing in a Hellenistic city exposed him to Greco-Roman philosophy, customs, and religious pluralism which were the elements that arguably influenced his later theological which are against every single thing God's people have ever been taught by God, his Son, the Prophets, and the Disciples have taught us.

1.3   Saul the Prosecutor

Following the death of Yehoshua, Saul either joined or was already a member of the Sanhedrin, a council of Jewish rulers known for their opposition to the Apostles and Disciples of Yehoshua. This group even advocated for the execution of Yehoshua's followers *(Acts 5:33).*

As a Roman citizen, he had the legal authority and mobility to persecute followers of Yehoshua beyond Jerusalem.

 Saul exceeded many who were the same age as him in the Jewish church.

Thus, Saul held a high status in the church which is why he was able to join the **Sanhedrin**. His high status was also an advantage when seeking approval from the **highest priest** to execute followers of Yehoshua.

The Sanhedrin was an evil group to be a member of. You may be wondering how in the world do I know that for a fact? Well, simply because **persecution** its self is evil. However, to persecute followers of God and his son is a combination of sinister and unspeakable evil.

To kill someone over the name of their God YHWH is the true definition of a **Martyr**. An example of a martyr is someone murdered because they refuse to call anyone else but YHWH Allah God and also refuse to deny him as the one and only true God and refuse to deny his law or break any certain law that results in their death.

A martyr is not Charlie Kirk or suicide bombers who kill themselves. To be a martyr a person must have been murdered over their belief in YHWH Allah, the God of Abraham, Isaac, and Jacob, or for refusing to do something that the Law of Moses commands them not to such as eating pork. Many people were killed in the book of **Maccabee's** for refusing to eat pork.

The book of Acts gives us a clear picture of who Saul truly was as a **prosecutor**.

He admits to being violent and hostile towards the followers of Yehoshua himself. He persecuted both men and women which left orphan children. That is if he did not persecute the children as well.

He would drag them right from their homes kicking and screaming whether they had children or not and imprisoned or persecute them.

Saul even approved the **stoning** of Yehoshua's handpicked **apostle** Stephen.

In the next chapter we will explore what happens during a stoning so that you can get an idea of the type of person Saul/Paul really was before we dive further into the true story of Paul.

Chapter 2: Death By Stoning

2.1   Introduction

To illustrate the severity of approving the stoning of an individual, this chapter is dedicated to explaining the process of stoning. Reader discretion is advised, as the content may be graphic.

The most recent documented case of death by stoning occurred in Sudan in 2022, involving a 20-year-old woman convicted of adultery. While rare, stoning remains a legal punishment in some countries, although it is often overturned before execution.

2.2   Why Stoning is So Vicious

Stoning is one of the most brutal and prolonged forms of execution. Unlike other methods that bring swift death, stoning is designed to inflict maximum suffering before the victim succumbs. The process is deliberately slow, ensuring that death does not come instantly. It is nothing more than curl torture inflicted on someone to ensure prolonged pain before actually dying.

2.3   What Happens to the Body During Stoning

1. **Initial Impact** – The condemned is often buried waist-deep or restrained, preventing escape. The first stones strike, causing severe bruising, fractures, and internal bleeding.
2. **Head Trauma** – As stones continue to hit, the skull fractures, leading to brain hemorrhaging and loss of consciousness.
3. **Broken Bones & Organ Damage** – The force of repeated blows shatters ribs, puncturing lungs and other organs, leading to slow suffocation.
4. **Shock & Blood Loss** – The body enters hypovolemic shock, where extreme blood loss causes organ failure.
5. **Final Moments** – Death usually comes from massive head trauma, suffocation, or internal bleeding—but it can take minutes or even hours.

The size of the stones is often regulated to ensure they are not too large (which would kill too quickly) but not too small (which would prolong suffering excessively). Stoning is also humiliating for the one being stoned since it was done publicly and allowed multiple people to throw the stones.

Stoning is widely condemned by human rights organizations as a form of torture and cruel punishment. Despite its historical and religious roots, many countries have abolished it, though extrajudicial stoning still occurs in some regions.

2.4   Stephens Stoning

The stoning of Stephen marks a profoundly tragic and defining moment in the early history of the Way—the community of believers who followed Yehoshua and his teachings, more on this in the following chapter.

As one of the first appointed true Apostles among them, Stephen stood out for his spiritual wisdom, boldness, and unwavering devotion to the truth revealed through Yehoshua. His public execution, carried out by enraged members of the Sanhedrin outside the city gates, was not only a violent rejection of his testimony but a chilling display of religious intolerance and religious indoctrination.

Stephen's final vision—of the heavens opened and Yehoshua standing at the right hand of Elohim—was a declaration that enraged his accusers and sealed his fate. Yet in his last breath, Stephen embodied the very heart of the Way: he prayed for forgiveness for those who cast the stones, echoing the mercy of his Master.

The evil of this act lies in its attempt to silence divine truth through brutality. And yet, paradoxically, it became a catalyst for the movement's expansion that would soon be destroyed by Saul when he becomes Paul.

Chapter 3: "The Way"

3.1 Introduction

To understand this section of the book and even the whole book itself you must know that Yehoshua and his followers were not Christians. In fact, Christianity did not yet exist. We will discuss much of this in the seek peek of Vol. III which is on the truth about Christianity.

For now though it is important to remember that Yehoshua and his followers were Jewish and began a movement within the Jewish community that was called "the Way."

While Saul was still going by the name Saul, he was among the Jewish leaders who were persecuting followers of the new Jewish sect known as "The Way," which is the actual religion that Yehoshua, the Son of God, founded. You heard me right Yehoshua was the founder of the movement within the Jewish community called "The Way," not Christianity.

Yehoshua and his followers were Jewish.

This is right in the Bible. However, many people over look this along with a whole lot more in the Bible because it is drilled in our heads that it is wrong to question the Christian faith. Preachers expect you to just go with what they say.

Well, I'm one Reverend that's going to break all the rules and follow God and his truth not man. It's time that the Christian community is told the truth.

3.2 Proof that Yehoshua and His Followers Were Jewish Members of a Sect Called "The Way" that was Founded By Yehoshua.

I know that many other Reverends and Preachers will be saying that I have no proof of what I am saying so I went ahead and listed some verses below that shows Yehoshua and his followers were Jewish members of The Way, not Christians.

📜 Key New Testament Verses Referring to "The Way"

1. Acts 9:1–2

"Meanwhile, Saul was breathing out murderous threats against the Lord's disciples. He went to the high priest and asked him for letters to the synagogues in Damascus, so that if he found any there who belonged to the Way, whether men or women, he might take them as prisoners to Jerusalem."

2. Acts 19:9

"But when some became stubborn and continued in unbelief, speaking evil of the Way before the congregation, he withdrew from them and took the disciples with him..."

3. Acts 19:23

"About that time there arose a great disturbance about the Way."

4. Acts 22:4

"I persecuted the followers of this Way to their death, arresting both men and

5. Acts 24:14

"But this I confess to you, that according to the Way, which they call a sect, I worship the God of our fathers, believing everything laid down by the Law and written in the Prophets."

3.3 Facts About "The Way"

- Yehoshua was the founder of "The Way"
- Yehoshua's brother Jame called "James the Just" due to his "Just" actions and Peter were the leaders of this new Jewish group after the death of Yehoshua.
- "The Way" was a movement within the Jewish community
- Members of "The Way" were of the Jewish Faith
- Members worshipped in the Jewish Temple
- Members followed the Law of Moses
- Circumcision was a requirement
- Members were followers of Yehoshua
- Members were persecuted by Saul
- Members were deeply rooted in Jewish traditions
- Members participated in Jewish customs and traditions
- Members kept the sabbath holy

Chapter 4: Why Did Paul Really Persecute Members of "The Way"

4.1 Quick Review and Introduction

We have learned a lot so far about Saul so let us review what we have discussed so far because this is a lot to take in, believe me I know.

Paul was born under the Jewish name Saul around the year 5 AD according to scholars. He never knew Yehoshua while he was alive and God nor Yehoshua ever mentioned him.

He was a Jewish Roman citizen and got along with the Romans well. Saul exceled in the Jewish church showing that he desired to move to the top of the ladder in the Jewish religion.

He was the youngest Sanhedrin member. Sanhedrin members were the leaders in the Jewish religion. These members began persecuting members of the Jewish group known as "The Way", a movement started by Yehoshua in the Jewish community after the death of Yehoshua.

Saul was very hostile and violent towards both women and men followers of Yehoshua. He even approved the stoning of Stephen.

In this chapter you will learn the difference between a Zealot and a Sanhedrin which will provide insight needed to understand the true reason of why Saul persecuted the followers of Yehoshua.

4.2 Paul Was Not a Zealot Persecuting for the One True God

Many believe that Saul was a Zealot persecuting for God. However, Saul was not a Zealot. Technically a Zealot was originally a member of a radical Jewish sect during the Second Temple period, known for their fierce resistance to Roman rule in Judea. Saul was a Sanhedrin.

Though the **Sanhedrin** and the **Zealots** were both part of the Jewish landscape during the Second Temple period, they were very different groups with opposing roles and **ideologies**.

🏛 The Sanhedrin: Judicial Authority

The Sanhedrin was the supreme religious and judicial council in ancient Judea, composed mainly of **Pharisees** and **Sadducees**.

It functioned like a high court, ruling on religious law, civil disputes, and even matters involving the king.

Members were typically elite, educated, and politically cautious, often cooperating with Roman authorities to maintain stability.

⚔ The Zealots: Revolutionary Radicals

The Zealots, which Yehoshua's disciple Simion was a member of, on the other hand, were a militant sect that rejected Roman rule and sought to overthrow it by force.

They viewed any collaboration with Rome—including by Jewish leaders—as betrayal.

Their tactics included assassinations and violent uprisings, especially during the First Jewish–Roman War.

Thus, Saul was a Sanhedrin which was not aligned with the Zealots.

In fact, the Zealots despised the Sanhedrin's willingness to work with Rome.

The two groups often clashed ideologically: one sought legal and religious order, the other armed rebellion.

What does this have to do with anything. Well, it shows us that Saul was not persecuting the followers of Yehoshua due to being Zealous for God like many people teach and believe about Saul/Paul. Saul was a Roman citizen who got along well with Roman authority figures. Therefore, God is not the reason he was ok with persecuting these members of "The Way."

4.3 The True Reason Saul Persecuted Members of the Way

The Jewish movement, "The Way" was threatening to the Jewish church because people flocked to it. This new sect in the Jewish religion was stealing the members of the corrupt Jewish church. The people finally were hearing the truth being taught from this new sect.

The followers of Yehoshua were becoming the new leaders in the Jewish community and that is really what pissed Saul off.

Saul desired power and control. He knew that religion was the way to gain power and control over the masses and he worked his ass off to make sure he was at the top of that religious ladder.

William Cooper an ex-CIA agent stated in his book A Pale White Horse that

"religion is but a tool to control the masses," (Cooper, 70).

Now, this new group was coming in and taking away the power and control that he had worked so hard for to gain. The Jewish high priest was actually the one responsible for the death of Yehoshua not Pilate.

Pilate washed his hands of Yehoshua's blood and attempted to let him go as a free man but the Jews was not happy with that because if Yehoshua was free to go then their power and control was still at stake and that is the true reason they killed the son of God. His blood is on the hands of the Jews not the Romans.

However, even after Yehoshua's death his followers still threatened the Church and Saul was determined not to lose the power and control he fought so hard for. He was going to kill every last one of them if he had to. That was until the Devil and his son offered him an even better deal.

Chapter 5: Yaldabaoth and Sabaoth's Great Masquerade

5.1 The Problem

In part one of this book, I told you all about the Bride Sophia and how she self-reproduced the being Yaldabaoth (the devil). Sabaoth (Satan), Yaldabaoth's son dethroned Yaldabaoth when he refused to acknowledge YHWH was the only God.

Since Sabaoth stood up for YHWH, YHWH lifted him up to the Earth's heavens and was put over all things in the Earth's heavens and on Earth. However, when Enoch, the Son of God and Bridegroom of Sophia, was transformed back into his true form, the form of Metatron, Sabaoth refused to bow to him.

He saw no reason to bow down to a human man because he did not know that Metatron was here before him and was the son. Thus, chaos broke out in the heavens amongst the celestial beings and Satan like his father, was dethroned and thrown back down to the earth.

After being thrown back down to the earth Sabaoth found his father Yaldabaoth. God swore to punish them very severely as soon as Sophia had her light back and could return ,. As soon as Sabaoth found Yaldabaoth the two of them got right to work devising a plan to prolong their punishment and bring their kingdom to earth where the two could finally rule.

If they came up with a good enough plan, they would be able to not only prolong their punishment but they would also be able to bring Satan's Kingdom to Earth. Yaldabaoth would finally be a god and Sabaoth (Satan) finally have the spot of a prince back, or that's what they thought anyways.

5.2 The Solution

In order to prolong their punishment that was awaiting them they had to trap Sophia here forever. God will not issue judgement until she has enough of her light back to come in the flesh in order to die and ascend to her rightful place in the heaven with her Bridegroom Metatron.

That means the Yaldabaoth and Sabaoth must dim the Brides light that is in humans. This must be done because only Godly bright light may be collected for the Bride to come back. So, their plan was to dim her light so it can't be collected which will result in her being trapped here roaming the earth in spirit unable to return home.

How did they plan on dimming the Bride's light in humans? There are two ways the Devil and his son come up with to accomplish that goal.

5.2.1 Dimming the Light in Humans by Making them Forget God

The easiest way to dim the light in humans is by making them forget God altogether. If you don't know God then you don't get into the kingdom nor is god with you. Thus, if they could make everyone on earth forget God then he would no longer be with people on earth. Therefore, they believed they could eliminate God completely by replacing him so that people would forget him.

However, they don't know God very well because if they did they would know that God would end it all before he let that happen. We know this is true because God did that very thing.

The devil and his son had already almost accomplished this goal once before in the days of Noah. As a result of the corruption caused by evil beings God flooded the world to reset it. Thus, it is idiotic for them to think their plan would work because it is God who has planned this all so that he gets his perfect family.

My favorite philosopher, a very well known and hated philosopher, by the name of Nietzsche said it best when he said "God is dead and we killed him." Because of this statement he made many called him a Nazi and atheist, especially since he hated Christianity as much as I do.

However, they were to unintelligent and brainwashed by Christianity to understand what Nietzsche meant. Nietzsche was not a atheist he believed in god very much but he knew that the Christian god was a fake. When he made this statement he meant the same as I do in this passage.

If the world were to forget God, the whole world, then it would be like god was dead to the world because we would be dead to him thus, by everyone worshiping the new Christian God and forgetting the true God in Nietzsche days they killed God in a sense. Not physically but the thought of him.

On the following page you will find a little card about Nietzsche to learn more about him and his claim.

Friedrich Nietzsche

My favorite philosopher is one of the most misunderstood and disliked by most philosophers, Friedrich Nietzsche. He is known for many famous quotes such as *"laugh now, cry later."* He is definitely known for saying things others saw as taboo to say which is why I relate to him so well. He is very well known for his hatred of Christianity which made him hated by many. However, His most famous, hated, and misunderstood quote is by far my favorite.

Nietzsche is most famous for the statement he made in his text titled *The Gay Science* about God, *"God is dead. God remains dead. And we have killed him. How shall we comfort ourselves, the murderers of all murderers?"*

Other scholars and philosophers believed him to be a supporter of the Nazi Party and an athesis due to this statement and his hatred for the Christian religion. But, he wasn't an athesis and he was not a supporter of the Nazi party he was actually against the Nazi party.

What Nietzsche stated was true in a sense and that is why God has sent me back from the dead, to expose the lies and sins of the Christian religion to the Christian people who are victims of the leaders and founders of Christianity.

What this brilliant man meant in his quote about God is that by the majority of the world following the Christian religion and worshipping the Christian God, they have forgotten the true Goad and the true son of the true God.

Although God cannot die, if the whole world forgets him and follows Christianity's Christ then we ourselves will be dead to God and thus, him dead to us. By doing this we are murdering the memory, worship, praise, thanksgiving, and faith that we once had in the ONE TRUE GOD, YHWH/ALLAH. Thus, those who participate in any worship of any God other than YHWH/Allah are the murders of all murders because they have killed God in a sense. Those who are meant to know truth will understand this.

The Brilliant and Brave Nietzsche: Misunderstood, Hated, and Labeled Insane By Christians, Psychologist, and Philosophers Loved and Understood by God

5.2.2 Dimming the Light in Humans by Corrupting Humans

Yaldabaoth and Sabaoth also planned to dim the light in humans through corruption. When humans do something with evil or bad intentions the light of the bride that is in them is dimmed. The one thing most people agree on is that the Devil, his son, and other unseen evil beings do corrupt people and cause them to do evil things. This is a self-explanatory topic that I'm sure you already understand. Now let's discuss how the two planned to carry out their evil solution.

5.3 The Great Masquerade Plan

In this examination of the Great **Masquerade** Plan, we won't revisit the well-trodden path of corruption, a truth universally acknowledged: that the devil and his **malevolent** offspring corrupt souls, casting a shadow over the **divine spark** within.

Instead, let's delve into a more **insidious** design, one that has as its ultimate aim the obliteration of humanity's connection to the divine—specifically, for those who follow the God of Abraham.

5.3.1 The Great Masquerade

Imagine for a moment that the darkest forces in the universe devised a master plan—not merely to corrupt, but to erase God from human consciousness altogether. This was the devious intent of Yaldabaoth and Sabaoth. Their strategy was beautifully sinister in its simplicity: distract and deceive by masquerading as the object of true worship, drawing souls in under false pretenses.

This calculated masquerade isn't simply about malevolence; it's an intricate dance of manipulation, where kindness is wielded as a weapon. Too often, we view the devil and his son as **embodiments** of pure **evil**—monsters lurking in shadows. But they are far more cunning; they are masters of deceit, skilled at whispering sweet nothings into the ears of the **unsuspecting**. By crafting narratives that cater to human desires and fears, they twist common-sense truths into a web of confusion, ensnaring society in a labyrinth of their making.

Your average person trudges through life with blinders on, utterly unaware of the grand deception orchestrated by these dark architects. Their plan is not a distant threat; it is a reality woven into the very fabric of our existence, a masquerade that plays out right before our eyes.

71

To execute their grand design, Yaldabaoth and Satan set their sights on hijacking the Jewish faith—a profound and **sacred** lineage—twisting its **doctrines** to create a counterfeit mode of worship that lures followers into their clutches.

By co-opting God's own son, they refashion him into a hollow distortion, a puppet dancing to their sinister tune. This new religion, masquerading as an authentic offshoot of Abrahamic faith, becomes a vehicle for their agenda: to trick the faithful into believing they are honoring the God of Abraham while setting the stage for spiritual **oblivion**.

They employed a simple yet terrifying tactic: feed the masses reassuring lies, enticing them with promises stitched together from their deepest aspirations. For those who dared to resist or question this new reality elimination was seen as a necessary step—an unfortunate collateral damage in their machinations, until the only beliefs remaining were own.

This **devious** plot unfolds across many layers and epochs, and it's in these layers that we uncover Paul's critical role—one that initiated the Great Masquerade which is now known as Christianity.

As we peel back the layers of this intricate deception, the shadows of truth beckon, revealing the profound ramifications of a faith reshaped by the very forces that sought to dim the divine light within humanity.

5.4 Why Paul to Kick Off the Masquerade

In the shadowy corridors of power, Paul emerged as the ideal **harbinger** of a transformative masquerade—one that would intertwine ambition, **manipulation**, and the mystique of hidden motives.

Just like the **archons** Yaldabaoth and Sabaoth, Paul was driven by an insatiable hunger for authority, desperately clinging to the control he felt slipping away. He loathed the followers of Yehoshua, seeing them as insidious thieves pilfering the influence and dominion he had tirelessly cultivated. After all, wasn't this the very fate that befell Sabaoth when the radiant figure of Metatron—Yehoshua in his truest embodiment—usurped his heavenly reign?

The stage was set. Paul found himself entrenched in a world rife with ambition and betrayal, where alliances shifted like shadows in the night. But he was more than just a mere pawn in this game; he was a **kindred spirit** to the forces of chaos.

Yaldabaoth and Sabaoth sensed in him a reflection of their own desires, resonating with their fractious aspirations for supremacy. If this was going to work though, Paul would need to learn that to gain true power, one must not brandish a sword but instead wield a silver tongue.

Rather than outright **persecution** of those who followed "The Way," Paul would need to utilize the potency of **persuasion**. The secret lay in crafting narratives that spoke to the fears and hopes of the masses, gently steering them toward his desired ends which is to turn from their old customs and traditions to worship this new counterfeit God that they would create to pass off as the son of God- Yehoshua, whom they would tell people was YHWH in the flesh.

Yaldabaoth and Sabaoth understood this dynamic; they'd long navigated the intricate dance of deceit and influence. Now, they turned to Paul, who stood at the crossroads of ambition and opportunity—a man who was ripe for a partnership shrouded in intrigue.

The air crackled with the electricity of possibilities as they approached him with a proposition. They knew, deep down, that he would be unable to resist their offer. For the Great Masquerade to be successful it would need many **orchestrators**, charismatic puppet masters who could manipulate the strings of faith and fear. This wouldn't be a quick mission or easy. It would take multiple power and control hungry people.

There would be massive bloodshed and worldwide confusion must take place and it would take very many years to unfold. However, they figured if all went right then Satan's Kingdom could be brought to earth and their punishment would be no more.

Chapter 6: What Really Happened on the Road to Damascus

6.1 Power and Control Hungry Headed to Damascus

While Yaldabaoth and Sabaoth were busy planning the Great Masquerade, Paul was busy persecuting members of "The Way." Stoning Stephen wasn't enough to satisfy him. Thus, he sought out permission to bring back more followers of Yehoshua to prosecute.

Paul received authorization from the chief priest to travel to Damascus with the intent of capturing more of Yehoshua's adherents. His plan was methodical: to track down believers in Yehoshua, chain them up, and drag them back for severe punishment—ultimately, execution by stoning.

The biblical narrative in **Acts 9:1-2** paints a stark picture of Saul's intentions:

> *"Meanwhile, Saul was still breathing out murderous threats against the Lord's disciples. He went to the high priest and asked him for letters to the synagogues in Damascus, so that if he found any there who belonged to the Way, whether men or women, he might take them as prisoners to Jerusalem."*

This passage tells us exactly why Paul was going to Damascus.

Further corroboration of Saul's notorious reputation is found in **Acts 9:13-14**, when Ananias, a disciple in Damascus, expresses his apprehension:

> "Lord," Ananias answered, "I have heard many reports about this man and all the harm he has done to your holy people in Jerusalem. And he has come here with authority from the chief priests to arrest all who call on your name."

This highlights the widespread fear and knowledge of Saul's cruel actions, even in distant Damascus.

6.2 What Christians Believed Happened on the Road to Damascus

Christians believe that Saul encountered the Son of God on the road to Damascus and that he was appointed an apostle by the son of God at this time due to Saul's own recollection of the event that is inconsistent in written text.

Saul states that while on the road to Damascus he encountered a blinding, intensely bright light that flashed all around him, which he adamantly proclaimed to be Yehoshua himself.

It is crucial to note that his traveling companions reported seeing nothing. They claimed only to have heard a voice. However, the specific words they allegedly heard were never recorded, adding an element of uncertainty to the truthfulness of their account.

Following this encounter, Saul declared a profound transformation. He asserted that he had been fundamentally changed by this "blinding angel of light." He publicly renounced his former mission of persecuting the disciples, proclaiming that he himself was now an apostle, dedicated to the very cause he once sought to destroy.

But was Paul really an apostle and did he really encounter Yehsohua? To figure out the answers to these questions we will first look at the true definition of what an apostle is and then we will discuss what truly happened on the road to Damascus.

6.3. Paul Did Not Have Apostolic Authority

Saul claimed a transformative experience upon encountering the blinding light, declaring he would no longer pursue the disciples and that he was now an apostle.

However, it is essential to consider that Yehoshua personally chose only twelve apostles. These disciples, selected directly by Him, were intended to be the sole true apostles.

Some may argue that Paul replaced Judas Iscariot after his betrayal, yet Yehoshua appointed Matthias to take Judas's place.

Below is the list of the twelve apostles chosen by Yehoshua, with the addition of Matthias following Judas's betrayal:

1. **Simon Peter** (also known as Peter or Cephas)
2. **Andrew** (Peter's brother)
3. **James** (the son of Zebedee)
4. **John** (James's brother, also the son of Zebedee)
5. Philip
6. **Bartholomew** (sometimes identified as Nathanael)
7. **Thomas** (also known as "Doubting Thomas")
8. **Matthew** (also known as Levi, the tax collector)
9. **James** (the son of Alphaeus, sometimes called James the Less)
10. **Thaddaeus** (also known as Judas son of James or Lebbaeus)
11. **Simon the Zealot** (sometimes called Simon the Cananaean)
12. **Judas Iscariot** (who later betrayed Yehoshua)
13. **Matthis** replaced Judas after he betrayed Yehoshua.

Yehoshua also had women disciples but the church hates to admit it.

In the days of Yehoshua and even before him women were oftentimes not given credit where it when they deserved to be given credit. However, it is undebatable that out of all Yehoshua's disciples the women, mainly the three Mary's, were the most loyal of all his disciples.

The three Marys' were the only disciples that did not deny Yehoshua and was even at the foot of the cross until Yehoshua gave his spirit up.

The main ten women disciples of Yehoshua are listed below.

1. **Mary Magdalene** – A devoted follower who witnessed the crucifixion and was the first to see the resurrected Jesus.
2. **Joanna** – The wife of Chuza, Herod's steward, who supported Jesus financially and followed him (Luke 8:3).
3. **Susanna** – Another woman who supported Jesus and his ministry (Luke 8:3).
4. **Mary, the mother of James and Joseph** – Present at the crucifixion and the tomb.
5. **Salome** – Mentioned as one of the women who went to anoint Jesus' body after his death.
6. **Martha** – Known for her hospitality and faith, she was a close friend of Jesus.
7. **Mary of Bethany** – Martha's sister, who anointed Jesus with perfume and listened to his teachings.

8. **The Samaritan Woman** – While not named, she became a witness to Jesus' teachings and shared his message with her community (John 4).
9. **The Woman with the Issue of Blood** – Healed by Jesus and became a testament to his power and compassion.
10. **The Widow of Nain** – Witnessed Jesus' miracle when he raised her son from the dead.

Yehoshua also had siblings.

It is rumored that Yehoshua had both brothers and sisters. However, we only know for sure that he had four brothers who are listed below. There are also some who believe that his siblings were his step siblings due to wanting to keep Mary a Holy virgin.

Little did they know the Hebrew meaning for the word virgin in the Old Testament Prophecies actually means young woman. However, of Yehoshua's birth story that tried to make sure Mary seemed Holy.

Although Mary was indeed Holy, she was not a **virgin** when she gave birth. She was probably a virgin when she got pregnant but she did indeed have intercourse and did so a few times. Below is a list of the known brothers of Yehoshua. It is rumored that he also had sisters as well.

1. **James** – Often identified as James the Just, who became a leader in the early Christian church. He is often called James the Just due to his fairness and righteousness. Many also know him as the father of the Church of Yehoshua. Though, he is not an Apostle he had Apostle like status since he was the brother of Yehoshua and one of the leaders of the church with Peter.
2. **Joseph** (also referred to as Joses in some translations).
3. **Simon**.
4. **Judas** (also known as Jude, who is traditionally associated with the Epistle of Jude).

As you can see, I have just given you many important names of important people that actually spent time with Yehoshua while he walked the earth in flesh. Out of all these people the now Paul, was not named once.

To be an apostle you have to be handpicked by Yehoshua himself. Yehoshua stated that there were only 12 disciples. Some may say that Yehoshua handpicked Paul on the road to Damascus but he didn't and Paul didn't even encounter Yehoshua on the road to Damascus as you all will see in the following section of this chapter.

6.4 The Truth About the Encounter on the Road to Damascus

The truth is Paul never encountered the son of God on the Road to Damascus. He encountered Sabaoth-Satan- the son of the Devil, Yaldabaoth. This was the moment Yaldabaoth and Satan decided to recruit their first orchestrator.

They are so good at putting on this Masquerade that they even shoved the proof right in your faces all in the Bible. However, they have become so good at putting on this show they get you to follow lies while also giving you access to the truth. The illusion they have created is just so hard for society to see through.

That is ok though, because I am not afraid to point the truth out for you all since no one else will. It's time to really look at what happened on that road to Damascus.

It states in Acts that on the way to Damascus, Paul a bright, blinding light that flashed. Yehoshua states that he himself saw Satan fall from the sky like lightening. Well, does lightening not flash?

Paul himself tells us that Satan masquerades around as an angel of light. Is this not what Paul encountered. An angelic being of bright, flashing light.

The name Lucifer alone should prove to you that Paul did in fact encounter Satan.

Lucifer is another name for Satan and the majority of people agree on this. The name lucifer literally means the shining one. The being Paul encountered shown so bright that it was blinding, well at least blinding to Paul anyways. The others with stated they saw nothing at all.

Now let's compare this to how others have truly encountered the Son of God. When Yehoshua appeared to his followers after he had risen, he appeared to them not as bright, blinding, flashing light but in spirit form.

They were able to see markings in his hands and feet which shows us he had hands and feet, just spiritual form hands and feet. He did not appear to them as blinding light.

Paul was blinding by the sight of the being he encountered. However, Yehoshua blinded no one he appeared to nor was anyone he appeared to harmed.

When Yehoshua appeared to his disciples all who were there saw him. When the being Paul encountered appeared only Paul could see it.

You see now. These are two totally different beings. The being on the road to Damascus had not one characteristic of Yehoshua when appearing to others. However, the being Paul encountered on the Road to Damascus relates very much to the way Satan has been described for years.

It was truly Satan that Paul encountered on the road to Damascus. This is the moment that the Devil and his son recruited Paul to Kick off this Masquerade by making people believe they should worship the son who would be morphed into Mithra by their later recruits in Vol. II.

Chapter 7: Paul's Invention of Christianity

7.1 Paul Didn't Convert, He Created Christianity

Many people believe Paul converted to the religion of the disciples but that's just not true. First of all, the disciples, Yehoshua, and Paul was all Jewish. Thus, there would be no need for Paul to **convert**.

The followers of Yehoshua were Jewish and participated in Jewish customs and traditions just as Yehoshua did. They worshipped in the Jewish temple. They followed the laws of Moses, worshipped only God, and studied the **Torah**. The Sabbath was Holy to them not the resurrection day.

When one converts to a religion they take on the beliefs, customs, and traditions of that religion. They do not change that religion to their own views they have created. However, as Saul, he kept the same Jewish traditions so there would be no reason for him to convert.

When Paul dropped his Jewish name Saul and took on the Roman name Paul, he also took on Roman customs and traditions as he was commanded to by Satan on the Road to Damascus.

The Law of Moses no longer mattered to him. He spread the false belief that we are all saved under faith alone which is the most idiotic claim I have ever heard in my whole life. The devil himself has faith that Yehoshua exist and so does his son Satan. However, I assure you that their belief in the son of God and God himself will not save them on judgement day.

As the author of James states in **James 2:19:**

"You believe that God is one. Good, even the demons believe but they still shudder."

There wouldn't even be no need for Judgement Day if our works did not matter to God. You can't just take a dipping in a pool with the belief that the son is God and expect to be saved no matter what you do, especially when the son isn't even God.

So, in this section of chapter 7 we can conclude with our very on logic and common sense as well as the words of God and the prophets, which includes Yehoshua, that:

- Yehoshua was a Jewish member of the Jewish sect called "the Way" which Yehoshua himself founded.
- Yehoshua was not a Christian since the religion did not even exist while Yehoshua walked this earth.
- The Disciples and 12 Apostles were Jewish members of "The Way," and this is proven in the book of Acts.
- The Disciples were not Christians
- Saul did not convert to the religion of the disciples because they were Jewish and so was Saul.
- To convert to another religion, one must change their views to the religion they are converting to not convert the views of the religion they wish to convert to. It just doesn't work like that.
- Yehoshua is not the founder of the Christian religion.

7.2 How Did Paul Start the Christian Religion?

In this section of this chapter, I will build on to what you learned in the last section by explaining how Paul actually started the Christian religion. By the end of this chapter it will all make sense.

Many of you that don't believe a word of what I'm saying probably will when I explain just how Paul tricked masses into becoming a Chrisitan with telling them what sounded good.

However, I will also point out some downright disrespectful things Paul himself wrote in the New Testament that will allow you all to see the Paul that hid behind the mask of kindness to get this religion started as Satan has commanded him to do in exchange for power and control.

7.2.1 Paul Feared by Followers of Yehoshua

Unlike what the lying founding bastards of Christianity has tricked people into believing, the followers of Yehoshua did not believe Paul's story or trust him. Although Paul's story about what happened after his encounter on the road to Damascus has inconstancies, he did eventually reach Damascus.

Christian leaders and preachers have the world thinking that Paul was just excepted by the Disciples once reaching Damascus. However, do not bother to inform you that the disciples did not just accept Paul. Once he reached Damascus, he told them all he was an apostle but they weren't buying his story.

Not long after Paul arrived in Damascus the disciples of Yehoshua planned to kill him **Acts 9:23**. Who could blame them for it either after all Paul had done to those they loved. Paul was informed of their plan though and managed to escape safely with the help of "his apostles," **Acts 9:25.**

What stands out to me about **Acts 9:25** and in other places in the New Testament is that it refers to Paul's people as Paul's disciples. The disciples of Yehoshua are known as the disciples of Yehoshua. No one calls themselves or is called a disciple of James or Peter.

Yet, those who travel with Paul are called disciples of Paul. Since Paul is claiming to be an apostle and disciple of Yehoshua why is him and his people not called that. It seems as if he just puts himself on a level of superiority that is as high as Yehoshua's and this is very disturbing to me.

When he reached Jerusalem, he was greeted by the true Apostles of Yehoshua in the same way. They feared him and did not trust him.

"When he arrived in Jerusalem, he tried to join the disciples yet they were ALL afraid of him. Not believing that he was a disciple." (Acts 9:26).

In the verse above you can see for yourself that the disciples of Yehoshua, the true Apostles, didn't think he was even a disciple much less an Apostle. Yehoshua had personally known his 12 Disciples and handpicked them.

It was them who heard his teachings from his own mouth. It was Yehoshua who explained to them that there were to be only 12 Apostles and that those 12 would be seated on 12 thrones in the Kingdom.

Now, here is this prosecutor of Yehoshua's people claiming to be an Apostle himself when he didn't even truly know what an apostle is and by adding himself as an Apostle it would make Yehoshua contradict himself.

Yet here this evil man was claiming to an Apostle to the two head Apostles, James and Peter. Paul claiming to be an Apostle and know so much more than these two men did about Yehoshua and his teaching in my opinion is disrespectful and disgraceful not only to the Apostles but also to God and his Son.

The Disciples knew that and knew something weird was going on so they got him away from their people and approved for him to go and preach to the Gentiles. However, they wouldn't chance jeopardizing the Gentile's salvation either so they sent missionaries behind Paul to preach to the Gentiles and this is when Christianity begins to form.

7.3 Paul Invents Christianity to Destroy the Church of Yehoshua

In this section of chapter seven we will look closer at the rejection of Paul from different groups. We will also be comparing the commands of God, teachings of the prophet, and the teachings of Yehoshua with the teachings of Paul. I will remind you all of what we as followers of the God of Abraham are supposed to believe to show you all how different true beliefs, customs, and traditions of God's people differ from the teachings of Paul.

Warning this section may make followers of Paul and followers of man angry. However, man and his feelings are not my concern. I will not be like other Pastors and Reverends who change Gods word to save the feelings of man. I am her to help save your soul not your feelings.

Although, I do understand how hurtful it feels to learn these things because I felt the same and I am still hurt by the lie that I was made to believe my whole life until my accident in 2018. So, yes, I too have feelings of hurt and betrayal caused by Christian leaders in me still to this day. I am outraged that these lies were drilled into my head since a child. So, lets get right to it.

7.3.1 The Rejection of Paul in Multiple Places by Multiple Groups of People

We already spoke about how the disciples in Damascus and Jerusalem rejected Paul and so did many other peoples. We must remember that although the Jews killed Yehoshua, Yehoshua and his followers were still Jews. The message Paul was teaching people was very different than Jewish beliefs and the teachings of Yehoshua.

In Acts 13:45-50 it states that when he began teaching his message in Antioch the Jews there contradicted him and that Paul felt insulted. The Jews there stirred up persecution against Paul and expelled him from their district.

Paul then goes to Iconium. In Iconium, according to **Acts 14:2-6,** the gentiles and Jews along with their leaders also did not accept or appreciate his teachings. They planned to mistreat him by stoning him to death. Of course, Paul heard of their plan and escaped.

After Iconium Paul then went to Lysteria where the gentiles, according to **Acts 14:11**, automatically associated him and his travel partner Barnabas with Zeus and Hermes. Now is the time to remember in the first section when I explained to you all that Sabaoth was Satan who also is called Zeus.

The people in Lysteria believed Barnabas to be Zeus and Paul to be Hermes. Barnabas was not Zeus though and he soon will have enough of Paul. However, it was Zeus (Satan) whom Paul encountered on the road to Damascus.

Hermes is known to be the messenger of Zeus. He was the Greek god of communication, travel, commerce, and trickery, known as the messenger of the gods.

In ancient Greek mythology, Hermes was a multifaceted Olympian deity celebrated for his speed, cunning, and versatility. He was the son of Zeus and Maia, one of the Pleiades, and was born in a cave on Mount Cyllene in Arcadia.

Paul also was delivering a message of trickery to create this great Masquerade for Zeus and Kronos (Yaldabaoth and Sabaoth) (The Devil and Satan). Thus, Paul does resemble Hermes and his mission.

In **Acts 14:19** that Jews from Antioch and Iconium came to Lysteria and that the crowds believed their message. The true Apostles were sending people behind Paul to straighten out his lies. Once the people in Lysteria heard the message of the true followers of Yehoshua they stoned Paul.

When they finally believed he was dead they dragged him out of the city. When Paul awoke, he was the disciples of Yehoshua standing around him and fled with Barabas.

The next uproar he would cause would be a big one and it took place in Judea which is now modern-day Palestine. There Paul got into a very heated argument with the disciples of Judea over circumcision; however, this is where the New Testament is a little in consistent along with the accounts of the Road to Damascus because in Paul's letter to Galatia this occurs in Galatia which is located in modern day turkey.

The argument got so heated that Paul was told to go to the church leaders in Jerusalem (James and Peter) on the matter. Once there they called the first council ever, the council of Jerusalem. However, I am not very convinced this took place and if it did I know that the outcome is probably not the true outcome.

It is believed that at the council there was more heated arguing about the matter at hand. Finally, Peter decides to end the whole matter by telling them to not bother gentiles with circumcision and he stated that the book of Moses is read every Sabath. This to me indicates that the Law of Moses should be what decides whether or not the gentiles should be circumcised.

What is even more strange is that the gentiles did not have a problem about being circumcised. Their problem was that Paul giving them false information was playing with their salvation which after all was what Satan has commanded Paul to do.

Not long after this incident Barnabas finally has enough of Paul and the two of them part ways after a heated disagreement about John *(Acts 15:39)*.

I have created a chart for you all below that lays all of this out for you to show you how many people and the groups of people that rejected Paul. This isn't all of them but its enough for you to get the idea.

📊 Chart: Groups Who Rejected Paul in the New Testament

Location	Group or Individuals	Reason for Rejection	Scriptural Reference
Damascus	Disciples of Yehoshua	Planned to kill Paul due to his past persecution	Acts 9:23
Jerusalem	Apostles of Yehoshua	Feared Paul, did not believe he was a true disciple	Acts 9:26
Antioch	Jewish community	Contradicted Paul's message, stirred persecution, expelled him	Acts 13:45–50
Iconium	Jews, Gentiles, and city leaders	Rejected his teachings, plotted to stone him	Acts 14:2–6
Lystra	Gentile crowd	Mistook Paul for Hermes, later stoned him after hearing true gospel	Acts 14:11, 14:19
Judea	Disciples of Yehoshua	Engaged in heated debate over circumcision	Acts 15 / Galatians 2
Jerusalem (Council)	James, Peter, and other leaders	Disputed Paul's teachings; outcome of council questioned	Acts 15
Final Split	Barnabas	Parted ways with Paul after disagreement over John	Acts 15:39

As you can see everyone didn't love Paul as Christians preachers make it seem. In all actuality no one that matters accepted Paul. In the next section of this chapter, we will discuss how Paul's teachings contradict the teachings of God, the prophets, Yehoshua, and the true 12 Apostles.

7.3.2 Paul's Gospel is Different than all Those Who Matter

To really understand the New Testament, you need to know the history of the books it includes. In the next vol. of this book, I go into very great detail on this subject. However, I feel you should know a little bit of this information in order to really see how Paul contradicted Yehoshua and the 12 Apostles and more importantly, God.

Not all of Paul's letters are written by him but the majority of them are. The one we will talk of the most in this section is the letter to Galatians which Paul himself wrote to the people of Galatia.

Paul's letters were written before any other books in the New Testament. Once you read his letters you will be able to understand that the letters of the Apostles were written in response to Paul's letters. Unlike Paul's letters, the letters of the Apostles were not written by the Apostles.

The Gospels were also written after Paul letters. Of the five Gospels, the book of Mark was written first. The others Mathew, Luke, and John were written based off the book of Mark. Scholars have no idea who wrote the Gospels.

However, during those days it was a tradition for people to attribute books to people that they followed or that inspired them. Thus, Scholars believe the Gospels were written by the followers of those men. The author of the book of Acts is also unknown.

Revelations I believe to be a copied from the book of Enoch and morphed into the Christian version.

All of the books in the New Testament have been Hellenized

The Worship of the Son of God

The very first commandment states that Yhwh is the one and only God and that there should be no other God's but Yhwh. Below you will find the exact verse of the first two commandments.

Deuteronomy 5:6-9

6 "I am the Lord your God, who brought you out of Egypt, out of the land of slavery.

7 "You shall have no other gods before me.

8 "You shall not make for yourself an image in the form of anything in heaven above or on the earth beneath or in the waters below.

9 You shall not bow down to them or worship them; for I, the Lord your God, am a jealous God, punishing the children for the sin of the parents to the third and fourth generation of those who hate me."

What these verses mean is that you are forbidden to worship any other god besides Yhwh no matter who that god you are worshipping is. Yes that means that you are forbidden from worshipping the son as well. This is why Paul chose to use the very son of God in order to make people forget God.

It is no secret that Israel has lacked in faith since they were first introduced to God after being freed from Egypt. Most of you do believe that the Old Testament foreshadows the New Testament so I want to remind you all of the bronze snake.

In **Numbers 21:4-9** we are told of how God sent serpents down to bite the Hebrew Israelites for speaking out against God and Moses when they became impatient due to their journey. The bites were painful and many of them died. They went to Moses and asked him to ask God to make the pain from the bites stop.

God then instructed Moses to build a bronze snake and to hang it on a pole which looks like a cross in many illustrations. When the people look to it with faith that it will heal them then they would be healed. It worked and the Israelites who did not die from the bites recovered.

Since they were healed when looking at this bronze snake hanging on the cross, they began to worship the snake.

Numbers 21:8–9

The Lord said to Moses, "Make a snake and put it up on a pole; anyone who is bitten can look at it and live." So Moses made a bronze snake and put it up on a pole. Then when anyone was bitten by a snake and looked at the bronze snake, they lived.

Worship of the bronze snake went on for a very long time. 700 years passed before a King would come and destroy the snake due to the worship of it.

In 2 Kings 18:4, King Hezekiah began major religious reforms and destroyed the bronze snake in the process due to the worship and sacrifice of the snake. You will find the exact verse below.

---

2 Kings 18:4

He removed the high places, smashed the sacred stones and cut down the Asherah poles. He broke into pieces the bronze snake Moses had made, for up to that time the Israelites had been burning incense to it. (It was called Nehushtan.)

This is so important to know because Paul has led many to believe that replacing God with the son by saying the son was God in the flesh has made people worship who they believe to be the son and forget God.

Many may think it's ok to worship the son because he is the son of God but it's not. Think about the story of the bronze snake and of Yehoshua.

The Snake was bronze and Yehoshua's skin was bronze as well. He was middle eastern and from what is now modern-day Palestine. Thus, like the snake Yehoshua was bronze.

The snake was hung on a cross made from a pole and so was Yehoshua. The snake heals when you have faith that it will and so does Yehoshua. People worshipped the snake and people worship Yehoshua.

God sent a king to destroy the snake and now God has sent me to stop the worship of the counterfeit son "Jesus Christ," which I will go into more detail about his name in the second volume, so that God and Yehoshua can both have the credit that they deserve and so that God and Yehoshua will be remembered again.

God is not three in one. The word trinity is never mentioned in the Bible nor is it even suggested. There is God who is Yhwh and he does have a counterpart whom he had made the son with. So, there is a family of three but the mother nor the son is equal to God. Yet all Paul preached about was Yehoshua whom he didn't even know while he was on this earth.

The true 12 apostles however, taught that Yehoshua was not God but the son of God and that God was the father of not only Yehoshua but all of us.

Yehoshua himself states that only our father in heaven is to be given glory in Matthew 5:16. He also reminds us that no one can serve two masters in **Matthew 6:24.**

Thus, it isn't the son that should be worshipped nor does he want to be. He didn't come so that he would be remembered as a god or to be worshipped. He came so that he may die in order to free our souls from the prisons of Sheol so that upon death we may go to God so he can say what to do with us in order to save those who are his and allow them to wait for judgement in Paradise instead of the prisons of Sheol.

The Law of Moses

Besides Paul using the son of God to make people forget god, he also stirred them away from following the laws of Moses which are Gods commands. Paul began preaching that we are all saved by faith not in God but in Yehoshua alone. There are very many things wrong with this view and it contradicts all the teachings of important people in the Bible.

In this section I will briefly go over some of these contradictions. I wish I had time to go over them in great detail but God is really pushing me to hurry up and get this volume of the book out.

After Paul went off preaching claiming to be an Apostle, he began encouraging gentiles who were willing to follow the law of God to not follow it. Matter of fact, he teaches that the law is no longer in affect. We are all saved by faith alone is the way Paul sees it.

However, God, Yehoshua, the Prophets, and the disciples teach us otherwise. The author of James tells us to be doers of the word and not hearers only in **James 1:22.** It then goes on to tell us in James 2:17 that faith by it's self without works is dead. Of Justification the author of James states clearly that a person is justified by works and faith, not faith alone in **James 2:24**.

Paul on the other hand, taught that by works of law no one is **justified Galatians 2:16**. In the book of **Romans** in verse **3:20** Paul states that by the works of the law no flesh will be justified in His sight; for through the law comes the knowledge of sin.

Paul also says somethings I find down right disrespectful about the law as well. Let us remember that although James himself did not write his gospel it was more than likely, according to tradition, written by one of his followers. James was Yehoshua's very own blood sibling. He spent his whole life with Yehoshua. He is also known as James the Just so I think it is safe to say that James knows a little about justification.

Paul in contrast knew nothing of justification being that he persecuted followers of Yehoshua for nothing. Remember Paul never spent one day with Yehoshua nor did God, Yehoshua, or the Prophets ever mention anything about Saul or Paul.

So, for people to ignore the whole Bible for the words of a Roman citizen who persecuted the followers of Yehoshua is still so crazy to me. Even I myself believed him and the truth is right in front our faces in our very own Bible but we trust those preachers so much that we believe everything they say.

Now, back to the story and the disrespectful things Paul wrote himself about those who teach the Law of Moses and those who follow the law.

Paul disrespects the son of God who taught that he did not come to abolish the law by stating in **Galatians 2:21** that if righteousness comes through the law, then Yehoshua died for nothing.

He used Yehoshua's death to led gentiles astray from following the law which Yehoshua himself taught us to live by. In Galatians 2:20 he even states that he himself has been crucified with Yehoshua which to me is ultimate disrespect towards Yehoshua.

He then goes on to tell gentiles in **Galatians 5:2** that if they get themselves circumcised then Yehoshua will be of no benefit to them. In Galatians 5:4 he tells the gentiles that those who are trying to be justified by following law are alienated from the son of God and that they have fallen from grace. Yehoshua himself followed law perfectly and was circumcised.

Paul even goes as far as cursing angels and anyone else who preaches opposite of him. What this means is Paul has cursed not only angels but God, the son of God, the prophets, and the 12 Apostles because they all preached that one must have both faith and works to be justified. He also wished that those who preached the law are mutilated in **Galatians 5:12.**

Of course, though, Paul contradicts himself about works and faith when it comes to justification. In Romans 2:6 Paul states that God will repay each according to their works and in **Romans 2:13** he tells us that doers of the law will be justified.

So, the big question here is why do people listen to a Roman citizen who persecuted the followers of Yehoushua, contradicts God and everyone else that matters, and can't make up his own mind. People have a way of following what sounds good to them and this is what has to stop. What hasn't been acceptable to God in the past is still not acceptable to him now. God does not contradict himself nor does his son.

7.3.3 Christianity Born

With this new teaching that is different than the original customs and traditions as well as the teachings on the Israelites we now have a new religion, Christianity. Christianity is based on the teachings of Paul not Yehoshua. As you can see Yehoshua taught a completely different message. He taught a Jewish message and was a reformer of the Jewish religion attempting to stop the corruption of the religion.

Christians believe that all are saved by Yehoshua's death if they believe in him. However, that is false. If all were saved by belief alone than even the Devil and his son Satan would be saved because they know and have faith that both God and Yehoshua exist. It was a demon who was one of the only three beings in the New Testament that identified Yehoshua as the son of God.

Christians believe that Yehoshua died for our sins as Paul taught them. However, this is false as well. God has been forgiving sins since life began and Yehoshua forgave sins in God's name while he walked this earth. Yehoshua died to free us all from the prisons of Sheol upon death so that we may go to God for him to say what to do with us until judgement day.

Christians call themselves a **monotheistic** religion but that is false and needs to stop trying to be identified as this as if the definition of terms don't matter. Monotheistic religions are religions that believe in one God and one God only and is the label of Abrahamic religions such as Judaism and Islam.

Christianity on the other hand believe in the trinity which includes three gods not one. They believe that God is the Father, the Son, and the Holy Ghost. This is false as well and all it takes is common sense to figure this out. Nothing can exist without God. Thus, the son is not God because if he were everything would have died in the heavens and on earth upon his death. God cannot die and does not change forms.

He is everlasting and unchanging and if it's the last thing I do or even if am killed trying, I will take my God back from God hijacking Christian leaders and I hope to wake up the Christian community so that they receive salvation upon death.

Christianity is a hypocrite religion that caters to the rich while ignoring the poor. They preach only God can judge, yet they are the first to judge and throw stones. The actions I have seen from Christians here lately have been anything but loving.

So, as you can see Christianity is a completely different religion that contradicts the teachings of God, Yehoshua, the Prophets, and the Apostles. The world has been deceived by the Devil and his son's messenger Paul from the very beginning. Christians will have no part in salvation if they do not turn from that devilish religion back to the religion of YHWH.

Chapter 8: Conclusion

This is where I am going to end **Vol.** 1 of ***God's Real Truth: Exposing the Great Christian Masquerade***. There is so much more to this story but it's so much that has gone on right up under our noses throughout history that in order for people to understand and meet God's time limit, it has got to be released in volumes. This first volume is the most important because it is God's real truth that he has shown me since my accident.

I am a seeing prophetess thus, what I say you will have not heard all of it before. Yes, you have heard bits and pieces of the things I've seen in these visions because they were a part of God's truth and at one time God's truth was known since we all started from the same two people.

Thus, many religions hold some truth the difference is some religions worship different beings in the story of Truth. Christianity is the main one. The Christian community does not worship who they think they worship and they don't know much of nothing about God's truth.

YHWH is the one and only creator and God. He in his loneliness wanted a family. So, he got to work on creating his perfect family. First the created Barbelo, his counterpart.

Barbelo then created the son that came to life when the spark of life went forth from YHWH. The son also created a counterpart, Sophia.

Sophia wished to create an offspring for the son but she did so without his help or approval and thus, Yaldabaoth come forth.

Yaldabaoth, also known as the Devil, was thrown to the bottom of chaos because Sophia thought she made a mistake and wanted no one to see. However, when she threw him down, she came with him as well due to him stealing the majority of her light upon birth since he was made by her alone.

Yaldabaoth saw no one but himself and believed he was God. He began to create all we see today and angels as well. His first creation was his son Sabaoth.

When he commanded that his creations call him God Sophia made herself known to him and rebuked him. She also asked for her light which he refused to give back as well as acknowledge that anyone was God besides him.

His son Sabaoth could see the glory of the true God though and dethroned his father with the help of some of the angels his father created. For his loyalty God sat him above the earth and allowed him to rule over all in the earth's heaven and all that walked the earth.

Sabaoth with the angels devised a plan to trick Yaldabaoth into blowing the light of Sophia into Adam whom they formed in their own imagination.

When the angels fell and Enoch was called up Sabaoth refused to bow to Enoch thinking he was nothing more than a human man. War broke out in the heavens and Sabaoth, Satan, was thrown back to the earth.

Once dethroned and back on the earth he sought out his father and when he found him they devised a plan to make people forget God and to corrupt them in order to dim their lights to leave Sophia trapped down her on earth to prolong their punishment and bring Satan's kingdom to earth.

It would take years of manipulation and the right people accomplish their plan. Paul was the first person they used to bring about their plan. However, over the years they have used many people and each volume of this book will expose more and more of these people. I'm writing this book as a command of God because they have just about succeeded in bringing their kingdom to earth.

I know a book like this is very dangerous to write and it gets more and more dangerous with each volume that will lead up until today's day and time. In volume two and all after I have true documentation to prove what I am saying even CIA documents which is what makes writing this so dangerous.

In the next volume I will be attacking the emperors, bishops, the popes, and the Vatican church as well as the churches today. You will see the real reason that we have had so many wars as well. These things are still happening today and being done against the last people left who know God's truth.

Jews are not off the hook either. I may have the Jewish star tattooed on me and it is the sign of God's people. However, the land of Israel that is here today is a big fat phony liar that is committing a genocide against the true Judah. We will get into this more in the following volumes.

We will also discuss how they have transformed the son of God into Mithra and how they have tricked you all in to worshiping a counterfeit of the true son of God. I am just a messenger though.

These are Gods words and what he has shown me. My job was to deliver you all truth but I will not beg you to believe me like Paul did. I will not put myself on a pedestal like Paul did either. I delivered you truth and you are free to do as you wish with the information as far as believe it or not believe.

However, I own copy rights to this book and if anyone is caught using these words without giving me proper credit or twisting my prophecies to make it fit your own twisted beliefs then you will be sued for all your worth.

I am taking back my God from all these fake ass religions. No one on earth besides the Muslim community at the moment has the right to claim the God of Abraham. The Jewish religion has become corrupt. The Christian religion is a damn lie.

My Islamic brothers and sisters tough, may peace be with you. Hold on a little longer, Allah does notice you. Allah thanks you for staying strong in your faith and the time has finally come for him to refine all those who don't believe, who have hijacked the true faith and who have committed evil.

Kent Kristmas you are a lying prophet who steals my prophecies and if it continues you will be sued especially your lil reverse rapture you stole from me and made it fit the Christian belief.

You see there will be a rapture and Christians will be taken up but they will be throwed in the lakes of fire and refined with the rest of the world while us who are chosen and know truth live for so many years in peace rebuilding Zion for the first time.

The Zionist here now are evil, fake, and not of God. They have counterfeited everything of God that is good and this is where it ends for them. I will take my God back and expose every last one of you down to family names in the different volumes of this book.

My hope with writing this book is that you all finally see truth. Its not secret that the world is in chaos all over right now in 2025. However, as more and more people forget truth and God the less God is on this earth. Today there is very, very few who know the true God. Thus, how can we expect anything less than chaos in a Godless world.

We can fix it though by remembering God. Remember the story of Jonah and how a city of barbaric people changed their ways after hearing about the true God. The city was then saved because it finally knew God.

My hope for this book is that many readers see truth in this book and come to know the true God the God of Abraham YHWH so that the chaos in this world comes to an end. There are some bad Christians in the Christian community and I feel betrayed and bullied by many of them.

However, there are good people in the Christian community who truly felt they were worshipping the true son of God and didn't know they wasn't supposed to it is them I am writing this for.

I am pissed with the founders and leaders of Christianity and with theologians who haven't had the heart to speak up about Christian lies.

I am angry with the Drs. of theology who have turned what was the study of God into the study of Christianity. Shame on you liars.

Chapter 9: Introduction to Vol. 2

In vol. 2 of God's Real Truth: Exposing the Holy Masquerade, I will tell you all the true history of Christianity. It will begin with the history of Christianity right after Paul.

This book is important because it will reveal how Christianity morphed God's son into the pagan god Mithra. This book will explain each and every detail of how Yehoshua's birth date, place, story, appearance, and more was changed by gentiles to match the story of Mithra.

We will discuss how the belief that Jesus is God in the flesh was shaped b

y votes of bishops the first "Christian emperor" called whose name happens to be Jesus Constine. When you learn this information, you will know why it is so important to call the Son of God by his true name Yehoshua Ben Yosef which translates to Joshua Ben Joseph in English just as Joshua from the Old Testament.

I will also be providing shocking proof to the claims I make in vol ii. You will easily begin to see how the devil and his son's plan has been orchestrated right under our noses for years.

A Message from God to the World

The following is a message to God for the world besides what you have already read. This is his direct message.

What is wrong with you all. Have you all lost your minds. Do you not care or love one another. Instead of moving forward and be more sinless you all have made an excuse to sin and treat one another horrible. Killing each other means nothing to you all. Did you give the breath of lfe for a person to live? I assure you, you did not.

All you contributed to a person was the flesh but it is the breath and light of God that makes the flesh work. Yes, the brain tells the body what to do but it is the light and breath of life that only comes from Me that allows a human to live, Thus, what gives you the right to take a life or deprive it from the rights that I God has given it.

You foolish fools. You think that you will get into my kingdom off of your faith alone but even the evil ones have faith. In fact, they have more faith than most of you. However, their faith will not save them because they did no works and gave no one any love.

What makes you think you are better than them when they are immortal and you are nothing more than flesh. I will not forgive them and I will also not allow anyone with no works in my kingdom.

Where have I once commanded or made a promise with you all that ended my law. Did my son not tell you all that he did not come to abolish the law? Did he not say that until earth and the heavens pass the law would still be in effect?

I assure you he did but you humans ignore Me, My Son, and my Prophets for the words of mortal men that don't even make sense.

You don't know history yet you open your mouths to try and state a case but you end up looking like lying fools. My truth has been watered down and changed around to fit what you all want it to fit and that stops now.

However, I did not hold it against you that all though you have the ability to learn truth and the book in your hands, that you were still too lazy to learn my truth yourself. So, I sent my prophetess to teach it to you and the way many have treated her is disgusting.

She has been called a witch, a liar, an atheist, and many more horrible slanderous names for preaching my truth that is in the very book that you all claim to believe and act as if I am the book itself.

Yet, none of you hardly ever open it and study it and believe words that's not even in it over words in it. Thus, you do not have faith or works. You Christians who think you will be first in the kingdom are the ones who will not enter. Being in church to worship someone other than me and not even knowing my name is going to get you a fast one-way ticket to those fiery lakes upon death.

A time is coming now when you will have to finally choose Me or man. Soon I am going to shake the whole earth. Many disasters will happen and no one will be left but my chosen who are not of only one skin color you racist fools.

A rapture will occur but you do not want to be counted among those who are taken up for they are not going to go have a good time. They will be burned and refined.

Those who are mine hold on a little longer. Those who are in Gaza who are originally called Judah. I see you and I have not forgotten you. Those who have stolen the name of my chosen one Jacob, they will pay for the illusion they have presented and for the genocide they have committed.

America you are not in the clear either. You paid for the genocide of my people Judah whom I loved. But all the pain you evil people have caused to the few who are left that are mine will soon have the same pain you have done to others come back to you. But my chosen they will not be touched.

No harm will come to them from any man, beast, or spirit. They will soon rule the world and leave in peace because I am about to wipe all evil and those who know me not from the face of the earth and then they will finally have a taste of peace once and for all.

Since you are too lazy to look for truth yourself, I have sent my prophetess to deliver it to you. This is your last chance to know me before disaster comes. My prophetess is only my messenger she has done as I commanded her and no man shall touch a hair on her head for delivering this message and if they try to harm her, they will fail and even greater harm will come to them.

This is your last chance to know Me and My truth. Who will you serve? God or Paul the messenger of the evil ones?

Those who are mine and in pain, hold on a little while longer. It is almost time. There will soon be peace. The circus this world has become will son end and you who are mine will build the true Zion because those who claim they are Zionist now are liars.

No Zion exist until I say it does and my prophetess has been sent to stop the corruption of the things you have all take from me and corrupted in order to confuse the world.

Those who have created these illusions you will soon suffer very greatly. I would have been better for you to have been eaten by a lion than what I will soon do to you for the sinister corrupted illusions you have created and given titles that only I am to assign. There will be no more warnings for you. Your illusion is over and you will so pay for its creation.

Yes, you Christians and False Jews in the land of Israel. You will soon reap what you sowed. There is no more playing with you. I am God not man and you have counterfeited all things of me that are good.

Now, though, my prophetess a woman who is truly loyal to me will destroy every illusion you have counterfeited and she will do so with words, not violence. All you have worked so hard for centuries to confuse the world and dim their lights is about to unravel now, one by one with each of my prophetess books.

I warn you again anyone who tries to harm her for obeying my commands will fail and what you try to do to her will come back x100 on you within a day. Not a hair on her head or a skin cell on her body shall be touched. The reign of you False Jews and Christians is finally over. Now, watch what you built come crashing down fast very, very fast as your lies and illusions are exposed.

Glossary

📖 Glossary (A–E)

Term	Definition
Abel	Son of Eve
Abomination	A practice or condition deemed spiritually detestable, often linked to unnatural unions or idolatry.
Adam	The first human in biblical tradition, formed from earth and animated by divine breath.
Angels	Celestial messengers and guardians who serve divine will and bridge heaven and earth.
Apostle	One sent forth with divine authority; in Christianity, refers to Jesus' closest disciples.
Archangels	High-ranking angels with cosmic duties—Michael (warrior), Gabriel (messenger), Raphael (healer).
Archons	In Gnostic cosmology, rulers of the material realm who obstruct spiritual ascent.
Barbelo	The first emanation of God in Gnostic texts; an androgynous Aeon embodying divine wisdom and glory. God's counterpart the mother of the Son, Metatron
Bloodline	A lineage of descent, often carrying spiritual, prophetic, or mythic significance.
Bride	Sophia.
Bridegroom	Represents Christ or divine masculine principle in sacred union.
Cain	Son of Eve; killed Abel out of jealousy, marking the first fratricide.
Celestial Beings	Divine entities dwelling in heavenly realms, including angels, Aeons, and archangels.
Celestial Realm	The spiritual dimension beyond matter, home to divine beings and eternal truths.
Character	The moral and spiritual essence of a being, shaped by choices and divine imprint.
Characteristic	A defining trait or attribute that reflects nature or purpose.
Chaos	Primordial disorder from which creation emerges; often opposed to divine order.
Christianity	Religion that worships Jesus
Convert	One who adopts a new faith or spiritual path, often through ritual or revelation.
Counterpart	A being or principle that complements another, often in divine or mythic pairings.

Term	Definition
Daughters of Man	In Genesis, mortal women who bore children with divine beings, producing the Nephilim.
Demon	A malevolent spiritual entity opposed to divine will; often tempters or deceivers.
Desire	A longing that can lead to divine fulfillment or worldly temptation.
Devious	Cunning or deceptive, often used to describe spiritual manipulation or falsehood.
Divine	Pertaining to God or sacred essence; embodying holiness and eternal truth.
Divine Spark	Power that comes forth from God
Doctrine	A set of teachings or beliefs, often codified in sacred texts or traditions.
Eve	First woman in biblical tradition, formed from Adam's side; mother of all living.
Evil	The absence or distortion of divine good; often personified in mythic adversaries.
Evil Spirits	Entities that corrupt, deceive, or torment; distinct from demons in some traditions.
Everlasting	Without end; eternal in duration and essence.
Enoch	Biblical figure who walked with God and was taken into heaven; associated with mystical visions and the Book of Enoch. He is also Metatron, the son of God in his true spiritual form.
Embodiments	Physical or symbolic manifestations of divine or spiritual principles.
Enchantments	Magical workings that influence perception, emotion, or fate; often tied to spiritual intention.
Esoteric	Hidden or inner knowledge accessible through spiritual initiation or revelation.

📖 Glossary (F-J)

Term	Definition
Firmament	The vault of heaven separating the waters above from the earth below; a cosmic boundary in creation.
Freewill	The divine gift of choice, allowing beings to align with or resist sacred truth.
Ghost	A lingering spirit of the deceased, often tied to unresolved purpose or ancestral memory.
God	The supreme being, source of all creation, wisdom, and love; omnipotent, omniscient, and eternal.
Gnosticism	A mystical tradition emphasizing hidden knowledge (gnosis), divine spark, and liberation from material illusion.
Harbinger	A forerunner or sign of what is to come, often bearing divine or prophetic significance.
Heavens	The spiritual realms above the earthly plane; dwelling place of God and celestial beings.
Highest Priest	The chief religious authority in ancient Israel, responsible for temple rituals and intercession.
Holy Scribe	A divinely inspired recorder of sacred truths and records all of mans deed, Metatron, the son of God.
Imagination	The creative faculty that bridges human perception and divine vision; a tool of prophecy and healing.
Incarnate	Embodied in flesh; often used to describe divine presence manifesting in human form.
Incarnation	The act of becoming flesh; in Christianity, refers to God becoming human in Jesus.
Insidious	Subtly harmful or deceptive; often used to describe spiritual manipulation or hidden corruption.
Interceding Prophet	A prophet who pleads or mediates between God and humanity, often to avert judgment or reveal mercy.
Islam	Abrahamic faith revealed through the prophet Muhammad, emphasizing submission to God and sacred law.
Jewish	Pertaining to Judaism, its people, traditions, and covenantal relationship with God.
Judaism	Ancient monotheistic faith centered on the Torah, covenant, and prophetic tradition.

📖 Glossary (K-O)

Term	Definition
Kindred Spirit	A soul with deep resonance and shared purpose, often recognized through spiritual or emotional affinity.
Kronos	In Greek mythology, the Titan who overthrew Uranus and was later dethroned by Zeus; associated with time and generational conflict.
Laws of Moses	Divine commandments given to Moses, forming the foundation of Jewish law and moral order.
Light	Symbol of divine presence, truth, and revelation; often contrasted with darkness or ignorance.
Lust	Intense desire, often carnal or misdirected, that can lead to spiritual imbalance or temptation.
Maccabees	Jewish rebel warriors who defended their faith against Hellenistic oppression; honored for courage and martyrdom.
Malevolent	Intentionally harmful or destructive; often used to describe spiritual adversaries or dark forces.
Manipulation	The act of controlling or influencing others through deceptive or coercive means.
Martyr	One who suffers or dies for their faith or truth, often becoming a symbol of spiritual endurance.
Masquerade	A false appearance or disguise, often used to conceal true intent or identity in spiritual warfare.
Matter	The physical substance of creation, often seen as distinct from spirit or divine essence.
Metatron	Mystical figure in Jewish tradition, sometimes identified with Enoch transformed; serves as celestial scribe and voice of God.
Mount Hermon	The mountain the Sons of God descended on
Mount Sani	Mountain of God
Nephilim (Giants)	Offspring of angels and humans in Genesis; beings of great size and power, often linked to ancient rebellion.
Oblivion	A state of forgetting or spiritual erasure; may symbolize separation from divine memory or truth.
Offspring	Children or creations; may refer to divine emanations, human descendants, or spiritual progeny.
Omnipotent	All-powerful; possessing unlimited divine strength and authority.
Omniscience	All-knowing; possessing perfect knowledge of all things past, present, and future.
Orchestrator	One who arranges or directs events, often behind the scenes; may be divine or deceptive.

Term	Definition
Paul	Apostle and early Christian theologian whose letters shaped much of New Testament doctrine.
Persecution	Hostility or suffering inflicted for one's beliefs, often endured by prophets, martyrs, and truth-bearers.
Persecutor	One who inflicts suffering or opposition upon those who carry divine truth or spiritual gifts.
Pride	Excessive self-regard; often seen as the root of rebellion against divine order.
Prophet	One who speaks divine truth, often calling people to repentance or revealing future events.
Prophetess	Female prophet; bearer of divine insight and revelation.

📖 Glossary (Q–Z)

Term	Definition
Sacred	Set apart for divine purpose; imbued with holiness, reverence, and spiritual significance.
Sabaoth (Satan)	Satan the son of Yaldabaoth
Sanhedrin	The ancient Jewish council of elders and priests who governed religious law and judged spiritual matters.
Secrets of Heaven	Hidden truths or mysteries revealed through divine vision, prophecy, or spiritual initiation.
Seer	A visionary who perceives hidden truths or future events, often through divine or spiritual means.
Self-Reproduction	The ability to generate offspring or emanations without external union; often attributed to divine beings or Aeons.
Semyjaza	Leader of the fallen angels in the Book of Enoch who descended to earth and fathered the Nephilim.
Set(h)	Son of Adam and Eve; seen as the righteous seed through whom divine lineage continues.
Spells	Ritual words or actions intended to invoke spiritual power or influence reality; may be sacred or profane.
Spirits	Non-corporeal beings, ranging from divine messengers to ancestral presences or malevolent forces.
Spiritual Gifts	Divine endowments such as prophecy, healing, discernment, or wisdom, given for sacred service.
Temptation	A test or lure that challenges one's alignment with divine will; often linked to desire or deception.
The Watcher (Sons of God)	In apocryphal texts, angels who descended to earth and taught forbidden knowledge, fathering the Nephilim.
The Way	Movement with in the Jewish religion led by Yehoshua and his followers
Torah	The foundational text of Judaism, containing divine law, history, and covenantal instruction.
Truth	Divine reality; that which aligns with God's nature and eternal wisdom.
Unchanging	Immutable; not subject to alteration, often used to describe divine nature.
Virgin (Hebrew meaning)	In Hebrew, often denotes a young woman of marriageable age; context determines spiritual or physical emphasis.
Yaldabaoth (Devil)	The devil. Self-reproduced by Sophia the Bride.
Yehoshua	The son of God, Metatron, in human form
YHWH	The sacred name of God in Hebrew scripture, often rendered as "I AM"

Term	Definition
Zeus	King of the Greek gods; associated with thunder, law, and divine authority in mythic tradition. Sabaoth

☀ Miscellaneous Glossary Additions

Term	Definition
Aeon	In Gnostic cosmology, a divine emanation or eternal being flowing from the source (often linked to Barbelo).
Anointing	A sacred act of consecration, often involving oil; symbolizes divine favor, calling, or empowerment.
Covenant	A sacred agreement between God and humanity, often sealed with promise and ritual.
Discernment	Spiritual insight to distinguish truth from deception, divine will from personal desire.
Fall	The descent from divine grace, often symbolized by Adam and Eve's exile or angelic rebellion.
Grace	Unmerited divine favor, healing, or empowerment; a key theme in redemption and spiritual gifts.
Holy Spirit	The divine breath or presence that inspires, comforts, and empowers believers; often linked to prophecy and truth.
Idolatry	Worship of false gods or misplaced devotion; a recurring theme in spiritual deviation.
Judgment	Divine reckoning or discernment, separating truth from falsehood, righteousness from rebellion.
Messiah	Anointed one; in Judaism and Christianity, the promised deliverer who restores divine order.
Mystery	Hidden truth revealed through spiritual initiation, often linked to divine paradox or sacred knowledge.
Redemption	The act of being restored or reclaimed from bondage, sin, or exile; central to divine healing.
Repentance	A turning away from error toward divine truth; often accompanied by confession and transformation.
Scroll	A sacred record or revelation; in your work, a symbol of legacy, truth, and divine transmission.
Seraphim	Fiery celestial beings who worship before the throne; associated with purification and divine presence.
Testimony	A personal or prophetic witness to divine truth, often born from trial or revelation.
Throne	Symbol of divine authority and judgment; often depicted in visions of heaven.
Transgression	A crossing of divine boundaries; often linked to sin, rebellion, or spiritual error.
Vessel	A being or object chosen to carry divine purpose, truth, or spirit.
Wilderness	A place of testing, transformation, or divine encounter—often symbolic of spiritual journey.

Charts and Tables and Photo

On the following pages you will find a couple charts thrown together and a real photo of an angel taken myself. God is real and the Heavens declare his glory.

Anointed and Called "Lord" in the Bible

Name	Role	Anointed By	Called "Lord"	Notes
(Yehoshua)	Messiah, Son of God	Holy Spirit (Luke 3:22)	Yes (John 20:28, Philippians 2:11)	Fulfillment of all anointed offices—prophet, priest, king.
David	King of Israel	Prophet Samuel (1 Samuel 16:13)	Yes (Psalm 110:1, Matthew 22:43–45)	Called "my lord" prophetically; type of Christ.
Saul	First King of Israel	Prophet Samuel (1 Samuel 10:1)	Yes (1 Samuel 24:6)	Called "the Lord's anointed" even after falling from favor.
Solomon	King of Israel	Zadok the priest (1 Kings 1:39)	Yes (1 Kings 1:43)	Revered as "lord king" by subjects.
Cyrus the Great	Persian King	By divine decree (Isaiah 45:1)	Yes (Isaiah 45:1)	Called "anointed" by God despite being a Gentile ruler.
Aaron	High Priest	Moses (Leviticus 8:12)	Indirectly (Exodus 4:16)	Called "lord" in priestly reverence.
Elisha	Prophet	Elijah's mantle (1 Kings 19:16)	Yes (2 Kings 6:12)	Called "my lord" by kings and servants.
Samuel	Prophet and Judge	By divine calling	Yes (1 Samuel 9:6)	Called "lord" by Saul and others.
Melchizedek	Priest-King of Salem	Divine mystery	Yes (Genesis 14:18–20, Hebrews 7)	Type of Christ; received tithes from Abraham.

📜 Prophets Of YHWH

Enoch	**Seeing Prophet Major Prophet**	~1000 BCE	The true son of God. Metatron in spirit form and sometimes called the lesser Yah. It is he who was in the flesh of Yehoshua and Enoch.
Abraham	**Major Prophet**	~2000 BCE	Covenant with God; father of faith for Jews, Christians, and Muslims.
Moses	**Major Prophet Seeing Prophet**	~1400 BCE	Led Exodus; received the Torah and Ten Commandments.
Samuel	**Major Prophet**	~1050 BCE	Anointed Saul and David; restored prophetic leadership.
Nathan	**Major Prophet**	~1000 BCE	Confronted David over Bathsheba; guided Solomon's rise.
Elijah	**Major Prophet Seeing Prophet**	~870 BCE	Opposed Baal worship; taken to heaven in a chariot of fire.
Elisha	**Major Prophet**	~850 BCE	Successor to Elijah; performed miracles and healings.
Isaiah	**Major Prophet Seeing Prophet**	~740–680 BCE	Prophesied the Messiah; visions of divine holiness.
Jeremiah	**Major Prophet Seeing Prophet**	~627–580 BCE	Warned of Jerusalem's fall; known as the "weeping prophet."
Ezekiel	**Major Prophet Seeing Prophet**	~593–571 BCE	Visions of dry bones, divine throne, and new temple.

Enoch	Seeing Prophet Major Prophet	~1000 BCE	The true son of God. Metatron in spirit form and sometimes called the lesser Yah. It is he who was in the flesh of Yehoshua and Enoch.
Abraham	Major Prophet	~2000 BCE	Covenant with God; father of faith for Jews, Christians, and Muslims.
Daniel	Seeing Prophet	~605–530 BCE	Interpreted dreams; apocalyptic visions of kingdoms.
Hosea	Minor Prophet	~750–720 BCE	Marriage as metaphor for God's covenant with Israel.
Joel	Minor Prophet	~835–796 BCE	Prophesied the outpouring of the Spirit.
Amos	Minor Prophet	~760 BCE	Called for justice and righteousness.
Obadiah	Minor Prophet	~586 BCE	Prophesied Edom's downfall.
Jonah	Minor Prophet	~760 BCE	Fled God's call; preached repentance in Nineveh.
Micah	Minor Prophet	~740–700 BCE	Foretold Messiah's birth in Bethlehem.
Nahum	Minor Prophet	~650 BCE	Prophesied Nineveh's destruction.

Enoch	Seeing Prophet Major Prophet	~1000 BCE	The true son of God. Metatron in spirit form and sometimes called the lesser Yah. It is he who was in the flesh of Yehoshua and Enoch.
Abraham	Major Prophet	~2000 BCE	Covenant with God; father of faith for Jews, Christians, and Muslims.
Habakkuk	Minor Prophet	~612 BCE	Questioned divine justice; affirmed faith.
Zephaniah	Minor Prophet	~640 BCE	Warned of the Day of the Lord.
Haggai	Minor Prophet	~520 BCE	Urged rebuilding of the temple.
Zechariah	Minor Prophet	~520–518 BCE	Messianic visions and apocalyptic imagery.
Malachi	Minor Prophet	~430 BCE	Last OT prophet; foretold Elijah's return.
Yehoshua (Jesus)	Seeing Prophet Major Prophet	~4 BCE–30 CE	Fulfilled the word of some Prophets; preached the Kingdom of God, saved our souls from prisons of Sheol to be judged.
Muhammad	Major Prophet Seeing Prophet	~570–632 CE	Received the Qur'an; restored monotheism in Arabia. Called Yehoshua his brother (spiritual/prophetic brother in God), Gabriel was seen washing a black clot out his heart with water from the golden vessel and put his heart back in his chest without leaving a scar.

The photo below is a photo of a star I took. This is photo prof that angels are real and they don't look the way that people paint them but they do match the descriptions of the prophets.

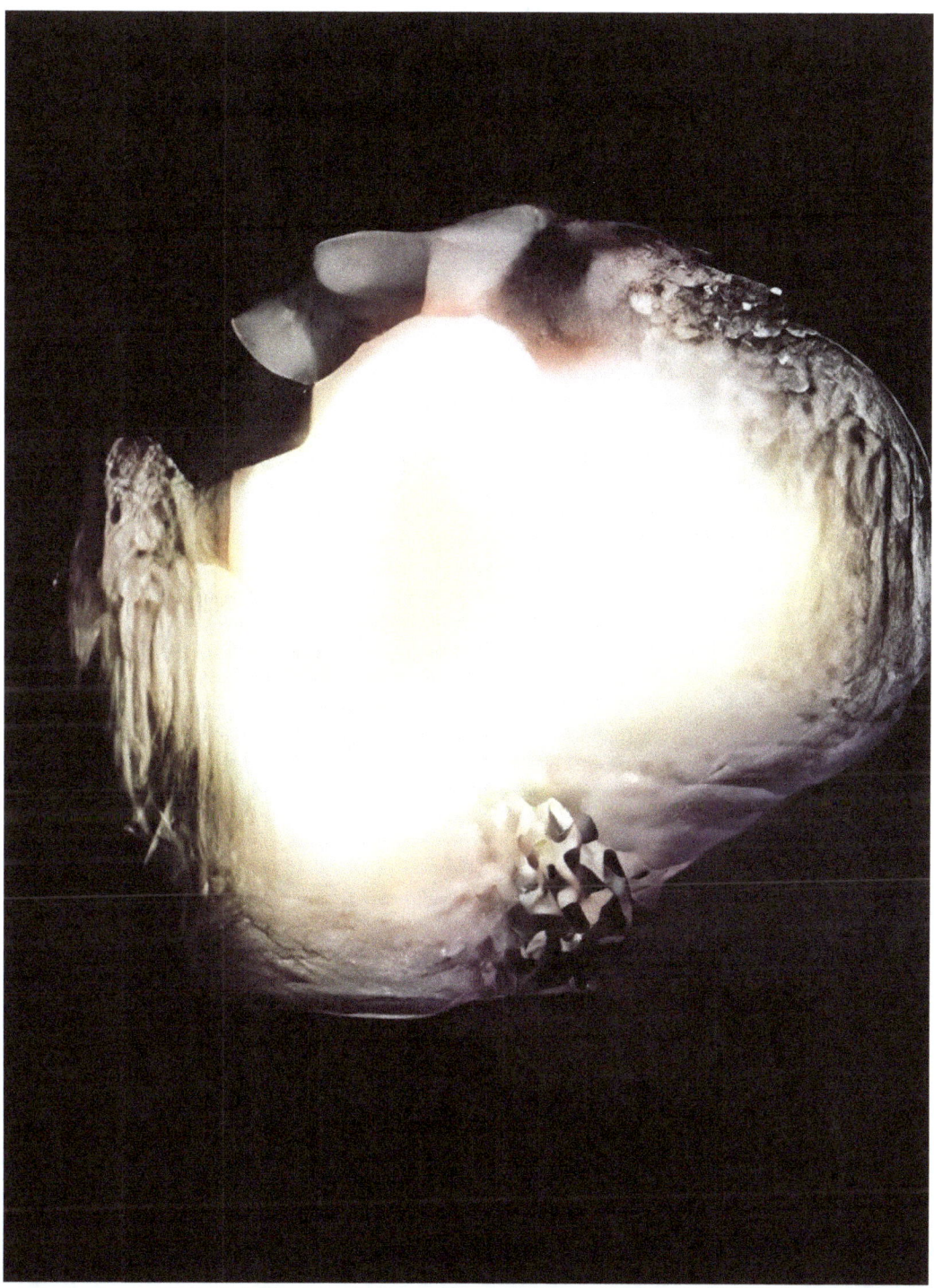

References

I planned to use many more references to provide more proof of what I am pleading with you all to understand about God. However, God has rushed me to get this book out and I have taken much longer than I should have due to nervousness. I understand I am speaking against the Christian Church, the most dominate religion there is in the world. However, the church is a big fat liar who has purposely deceived the world in the most sinister way. I never planned on preaching or speaking against God but he had other plans and who am I to argue with my maker. God told me that those who are supposed to understand will understand

1. Cooper, William. *Behold a Pale Horse*. Light Technology Publishing, 1991.
2. Soards, Marion L. *The Apostle Paul*. Paulist Press, 1989
3. *She Reads Truth Christian Bible Bible*.

Message me with any questions you may have no matter the day or time. Remember there are no stupid questions.

Email: tabootruths.ka@gmail.com

Website Links: https://authorkristyanders.wixsite.com/taboo-truths

www.tabootruths.org

NOTES